CONVOY
PROTECTION

CONVOY
PROTECTION
The Defence of Seaborne Trade

PAUL KEMP

ARMS AND
ARMOUR

Arms and Armour Press
A Cassell Imprint
Villiers House, 41–47 Strand, London WC2N 5JE.

Distributed in the USA by Sterling Publishing Co. Inc.,
387 Park Avenue South, New York, NY 10016-8810.

Distributed in Australia by Capricorn Link (Australia)
Pty. Ltd, P.O. Box 665, Lane Cove, New South Wales
2066.

British Library Cataloguing-in-Publication Data: a
catalogue record for this book is available from the
British Library

ISBN 1-85409-037-2

Typeset by Ronset Typesetters Ltd., Darwen,
Lancashire.

Printed and bound in Great Britain by Hartnolls Ltd.,
Bodmin, Cornwall.

CONTENTS

ACKNOWLEDGMENTS

It gives me great pleasure to express my gratitude to those who have helped in the research for this book: Margaret Bidmead of the Royal Navy Submarine Museum; Colin Bruce and Allison Duffield of the Department of Printed Books, the Imperial War Museum; Bob Galbani of the US Submarine Memorial and Museum at New London, Connecticut; Ed Foinney of the US Naval Historical Center, Washington; Arnold Hague and M. McAloon of the Naval Historical Branch at the Ministry of Defence; V. E. Tarrant; and Karl Wahnig. Any errors in what follows are exclusively my responsibility.

Paul Kemp

CHAPTER ONE

Essential Service or Irregular Operation?

I consider the protection of trade the essential service that can be performed. —
Horatio, Lord Nelson

T HE THEORIES asserting the supremacy of the capital ship in naval
warfare advocated by the American historian Alfred Thayer Mahan
at the end of the nineteenth century in his books *The Influence of Sea
Power upon History 1660–1783* and *The Influence of Sea Power upon the French
Revolution and Empire 1793–1812* have dominated naval thinking in the
twentieth century. As a result an over-emphasis has been placed on the
development and operation of large battle-fleets while commerce raiding and,
more importantly, the defence of seaborne trade against a *guerre de course*,
which Mahan described as an irregular secondary operation, have been
neglected. The fascination with 'the big ship' continues today despite the fact
that submarine interdiction of seaborne trade came within measurable
distance of victory in the Atlantic in the First World War and brought Japan
to her knees in the Second.

During the First World War Britain, and her allies, withstood the
onslaught of the German U-boats through the introduction of a convoy
system and other measures, although the German campaign of unrestricted
submarine warfare came close to success. On the other side of the world in
the Second World War, Japan neglected to develop any coherent strategy of
trade defence and paid the price. By September 1945 Japan's merchant
marine had been ravaged by American submarines and, whatever her
military capability may have been, she lacked the logistic resources either to
maintain her overseas empire or to keep her war industries supplied with
strategic materials. Trade protection enabled Britain to survive in the First
World War; lack of it caused Japan's war economy to collapse in the Second.
In both cases the key to the success or failure of trade protection policies lay
with the convoy system. Other aspects—the development of new weapons
and countermeasures, intelligence, and the mass production of escorts and
merchant ships—were important, but the convoy system was the lynchpin of
victory. The big battle-fleets in which Britain and Japan had invested so
much in the way of manpower and resources had little to do with either
campaign.

The convoy enjoys a prominent, though perhaps little known, role in naval
history. The first role of the earliest fighting ships, often little more than

armed merchantmen themselves, was the protection of merchant shipping from the privations of the enemy fleet or individual raiders. The convoy, or group of merchant ships sailing together, was seen as the best and most efficient way of protecting merchant shipping. The first record of any convoy appears in 1215 when King John took his army to Flanders in a 500-ship convoy. Likewise in 1346 King Edward III organized a 600-ship convoy, while Henry V used a 1,200-ship convoy to take his army to France in 1415 for the campaign which culminated in the victory at Agincourt. Indeed, Henry V's use of the convoy, with points of assembly and dispersal for the ships involved, would have been familiar to any convoy commodore of the First or Second World War.

Britain was not the only power to appreciate the virtues of the convoy system. Spain depended on the safe carriage of gold and precious metals from her conquests in South America and the Caribbean for the maintenance of her European empire. The ships carrying this cargo, known as the *Flota*, were valuable and could not be allowed to fall victim to the nefarious activities of English privateers. Accordingly the Spanish devised means of protecting their treasure ships. Regular patrolling of the routes used by the *Flota* was one early option, but in 1526 treasure ships were forbidden to sail independently and a convoy system was established, with close and ocean escorts. In 1589 Sir Richard Grenville was possibly the first of a series of naval commanders throughout history who attempted an attack on a convoy and had cause to regret his decision: his flagship *Revenge* was battered to a hulk by the escorts. Thus was emphasized one maxim of naval warfare which was to become frighteningly true in both world wars, namely that an attack on a convoy is one of the most hazardous naval operations any commander can attempt.

From the Dutch Wars of the mid-seventeenth century until the final defeat of Napolean in 1815 the convoy was at the very centre of naval warfare. Many of the great sea fights whose names echo in the history books are convoy actions, the battle known as the Glorious First of June (1794) being a particularly relevant example. The battle arose out of an English attempt to block the passage to France of an immense grain convoy which had sailed from the Chesapeake. Admiral Earl Howe, the British commander, brought about a general fleet action and succeeded in capturing six French ships of the line while another foundered. The French suffered a tactical defeat but succeeded in their primary object, the safe arrival of the convoy.

The convoy system reached its zenith during the Revolutionary and Napoleonic Wars. Although the French and Spanish fleets in themselves were not a great threat to British commerce, the depredations of French privateers were. Fast, well-armed, and operating for profit rather than out of altruism, French privateers constituted a considerable menace to the merchant ships bringing the food and supplies which England needed for carrying on the war. A convoy system was evolved to meet the threat. Ships would assemble off the Isle of Wight, regardless of destination, and, escorted by a strong force including ships of the line, proceed down-channel to the 'Soundings' (100-fathom line). There the ships would disperse and split into smaller convoys each bound for a particular destination and each with its own passage escort. Convoys ran on monthly intervals to North and South America, the West Indies, the Cape of Good Hope and beyond. Two- to three-week intervals were the rule for the Baltic convoys—Admiral Saumarez once brought a convoy of 1,000 head of sail out of the Baltic—while coastal convoys around Britian and to Ireland and the Channel Islands ran at weekly intervals. The convoy system was popular with merchant seamen and owners alike: no surer proof of the system's success can be found than in the fact that in 132 recorded convoys between 1793 and 1797, 5,827 ships were convoyed and only 35 (0.6 per cent) were taken by enemy privateers. The London insurance market recognized the success of convoy and charged higher premiums—often 30 to 40 per cent higher—on those ships which chose to sail independently. In 1798 the Compulsory Convoy Act was passed which empowered the Admiralty to enforce the convoy system on all ocean-going ships. While the great victories like those at St Vincent (14 February 1797) and Trafalgar (21 October 1805) stole the headlines, the convoy system went on quietly working, assuring Britain's economic ability to pursue the war to its victorious conclusion.

Convoy worked and was seen to work. It was nothing more than the classic application of the principles of concentration and economy of force. Yet, only seventy years after Trafalgar, 'convoy' was a discredited word in the naval vocabulary and the lessons of history were all but forgotten. It would take a war in which Britain came close to seeking a negotiated settlement before the convoy system would be given a reprieve.

Why was convoy so quickly discredited? It would be facile to suggest that the Royal Navy simply forgot the lessons of history as they accepted the pace of technological change by discarding old sailing ships in favour of steam, but there is a ring of truth in the argument. A more fundamental reason lies in the preoccupation of the British with their Empire, a preoccupation which grew to near obsession as the nineteenth century neared its end. Look at any map of the period and the sea lanes will be marked out in red as if they represented tangible routes which could be physically protected. Naval thinking began to move toward guarding the sea lanes rather than ships.

The change in emphasis is hard to understand given the outstanding success of the convoy in the Napoleonic Wars, but it is even more difficult to comprehend when considered in the light of Britain's growing overseas empire in the nineteenth century. As Britain's prosperity grew so did her dependence on seaborne trade. British factories needed imported raw materials, her population was fed on imported grain and her prosperity depended on exports and the ships that carried them. France was Britain's most likely adversary throughout much of the nineteenth century and the

French had grasped the nature of the British weakness. As early as 1851 a French naval commission had recommended that, if a war broke out, 'we must at its very commencement strike at the trade of the enemy. To strike at the trade of England is to strike her at the heart.'[1] The young and aggressive thinkers of the *Jeune Ecole* went along the same lines, believing in a *guerre de course* using cruisers to destroy merchant ships.

Yet a long period of peace with no serious naval threat wove its spell of spreading a false calm. In 1872 the Compulsory Convoy Act was repealed. In December 1874 the Admiralty conducted a review of their war plans which was to exercise a mesmerizing influence on attitudes to trade protection until well into the twentieth century. The Admiralty saw the empire as a single entity bound together by the sea lanes, which were seen as a tangible means of communication. If these routes were severed, then Britain would be ruined. In May 1885 the Foreign Intelligence Committee considered the whole issue of trade protection but convoy was not included as an option in their discussions. Blockade of the enemy's bases was to be left to the battle-fleet while cruisers patrolled the sea lanes. In thinking thus the Admiralty had missed the wood for the trees: it was not the sea lanes that needed protection but the ships carrying their valuable cargoes which sailed along them.

Mahan's theories of sea power only served to confirm what was already being held as sound strategic doctrine. His famous description of the Royal Navy during the Napoleonic Wars—'those distant, storm-beaten ships on which the Grand Army never looked stood between it and domination of the world'[2]—only served to emphasize the role of the battle-fleet while the *guerre de course* and the means of defence against such a campaign were regarded as a

> . . . secondary operation of naval war . . . but regarded as a primary and fundamental measure sufficient in itself to crush the enemy, it is probably a delusion.[3]

Yet Mahan recognized the value of convoy. Writing in *The Influence of Sea Power upon the French Revolution and Empire 1793–1812*, he observed that

> . . . the result of the convoy system . . . warrants the inference that, when properly systematized and applied, it will have more success as a defensive measure than hunting for individual marauders—a process which, even when thoroughly planned, still resembles looking for a needle in a haystack.[4]

The important point here is Mahan's use of words 'defensive measure'. By the end of the nineteenth century it was accepted that assigning warships to

---

[1] J. Winton, *Convoy: The Defence of Sea Trade 1890–1990* (London: Michael Joseph, 1983), p.45.

[2] J. Terraine, *Business in Great Waters: The U-boat Wars 1916–45* (London: Leo Cooper, 1989), p.45.

[3] A. T. Mahan, *The Influence of Sea Power on the French Revolution and Empire* (Boston, 1894), p.216.

[4] *Ibid.*, p.217.

convoy duty was to act 'defensively', which was intrinsically bad, while patrolling the sea lanes was good because it was acting 'offensively'.

By the twentieth century the naval scene was dominated by the big-gun battleship and plans for a decisive naval engagement. Trade protection was relegated to the sidelines. The battle-fleet would exercise the traditional role of blockade while a large number of cruisers (requiring an equally large number of overseas bases to support them) linked together by wireless telegraphy (W/T) would patrol the sea lanes to clean up any marauders. The weakness of this argument was demonstrated, though the lessons were not taken to heart, during the 1906 Manoeuvres. Blue Fleet's cruisers conducted a *guerre de course* against Red Fleet's merchant ships. Although Blue Fleet was adjudged to have 'lost', some very important conclusions were there to be drawn by the intelligent observer. Of the 400 merchant ships which passed through the area, some 94 were liable to attack: of these, 52 (i.e. more than half) were adjudged to have been 'sunk'—all by small cruisers of groups or destroyers.

Another important development in the early twentieth century was the shift in the pattern of alliances as Germany supplanted France as Britain's most likely adversary. In 1897 *Kaiser* Wilhelm II appointed *Admiral* Alfred von Tirpitz as his Navy Minister and there followed a remarkable change in German naval policy. Tirpitz saw a large navy as essential if Germany were to achieve her proper position among world powers, and with the passing of the Naval Law in 1898 he set about creating a fleet to rival that of the Royal Navy. Space precludes a discussion of the naval race between Britain and Germany which preceded the Great War. What is of more importance here is the effect of the new threat on the arguments surrounding trade protection. In 1913 Britain imported 80 per cent of her wheat and 50 per cent of her meat. The Industrial Revolution had stripped the land of labour and the country depended on imports of food in return for exports of manufactured goods. Well over one million people, for example, worked in the textile industry, nearly all of whose products went for export. Nearly 50 per cent of the pig iron produced in Britain was made from imported ore and, more importantly, the oil which powered the Navy's newest and most powerful ships, the *Queen Elizabeth* class 'super-dreadnoughts', all had to be imported.

Those writers and naval thinkers considering Britain's position found little to alarm them. In an article by Commander K. C. B. Dewar RN, published in the *Naval Review* of 1914 and dealing with the question of the effect of foreign trade on naval policy, the potential enemy was clearly seen as Germany. Dewar recommended the old recipe of blockading the enemy fleet in its harbours while patrolling the sea routes with cruisers. In a supplementary article by Commander E. V. F. R. Dugmore, convoy was not mentioned. Since steamers were not bound by the wind as were the old sailing ships, they could 'escape in any direction' and their Masters would be in receipt of accurate intelligence, through W/T, and would be able to avoid areas where raiders were known to be operating. Moreover, enemy commerce raiders would be hampered by a lack of bases, difficulties over supplies of coal, an inability to risk an engagement with an equal force for fear of damage, and lack of accurate intelligence. Thus the raiders would swiftly fall victim to the large number of British cruisers patrolling the seas, and Dugmore felt safe in concluding that 'we are justified in believing convoy, as a regular system, obsolete'.

Given the strength of the Royal Navy in the years immediately before the First World War, Dugmore's arguments appear to carry some weight. Any spectator of the annual Fleet Reviews at Spithead seeing the massed ranks of warships would have thought that both the strategy of blockade and patrolling the sea routes could be easily maintained. But the possibility that the enemy battle-fleet would remain in harbour, acting as a 'fleet in being' and tying down the British ships while conducting a *guerre de course* using another weapon, was not considered. Indeed, had Germany stuck to using surface raiders, either cruisers like the *Emden* or converted merchantmen like the *Wolf* or *Möwe*, then Dugmore's arguments might have carried the day since these ships, though successful in a limited way, all suffered from the problems outlined above. But in the submarine Germany possessed a new weapon which gave commerce raiding a new dimension.

The submarine has a naval pedigree going back to the seventeenth century but it was not until the first decade of the twentieth that it entered the ranks of the world's navies in any number. These small vessels were regarded with a mixture of loathing and suspicion since they threatened to overturn the supremacy of the big battle-fleet. By 1912 Britain had the largest and technically most advanced fleet in the world, with France and America following behind. Germany entered the submarine business late: it was not until 1905 that Krupps received the order for the first U-boat. Despite the effort and expense devoted to submarine development before the First World War, the naval powers had little idea of how these new weapons were to be employed.

In Britain there were some who prophesied that Germany would use her U-boats against commerce. That maverick admiral Admiral Sir John ('Jacky') Fisher, who was a supporter of the submarine, argued such a scenario in a paper written in 1913, but his argument was treated with contempt by both the political and the professional leadership of the day. Ironically the First Lord of the Admiralty at the time who dismissed Fisher's hypothesis so calmly was none other than Winston Churchill, who would later go on record and admit that the only thing that 'really frightened me in the war was the U-boat peril'.

What was the position of this new weapon in regard to international law on commerce raiding? In theory, submarines were bound by the same rules as surface warships, which meant that they had to abide by the provisions of the Declaration of London of 1909—an instrument whose effectiveness was blunted by the fact that none of the signatories ratified it (although the Asquith Government announced that Britain would adhere to its provisions). The Declaration of London defined those goods which could legally be seized by a belligerent and confirmed that enemy merchant ships could legally be sunk or taken as prizes. However, cargoes consigned to a belligerent country but carried in neutral vessels were far more problematic. Three categories were defined for such cargoes:

1. Absolute Contrabrand. A very short list of materials directly associated with the war effort and whose destination was enemy territory. These could seized outright.

2. Conditional Contrabrand. Goods which might or might not be associated with the war effort (fuel and fodder are two examples). Such goods could only be seized if they were clearly destined for an enemy port. If such a cargo were consigned to a neutral port, then the cargo was inviolate. Considering that Holland and Denmark would be neutral in the Great War and that Rotterdam and Copenhagen were centres of German commerce, conditional contrabrand was, clearly, going to be an area of contention.

3. Free Goods. The most contentious area of all and comprising goods which were above seizure even though they included items such as metal ores, rubber, textiles and items of machinery, all of which were clearly relevant to the war effort.

One thing, though, was apparent. To establish the nature of a cargo carried by a merchantman, be she a belligerent or a neutral, a boarding party would have to board the ship and examine her papers, perhaps even the cargo. If the cargo were declared to be contrabrand then a prize crew would have to take the ship to a British port where the cargo would be purchased before the merchant ship could be released. This complicated procedure was perfectly feasible for a cruiser which carried a fairly large crew and could always accommodate extra officers and men for prize crews, but it was clearly impractical for a submarine, as was realized by Admiral 'Jacky' Fisher, who while in retirement wrote to Winston Churchill in 1913 that the submarine

> . . . cannot capture the merchant ship; she has no spare hands to put a prize crew on board . . . she cannot convoy her into harbour . . . There is nothing else the submarine can do except sink her capture . . . [this] is freely acknowledged to be an altogether barbarous form of warfare [but] the essence of war is violence, and moderation in war is imbecility.[5]

To the naval mind, the idea that a submarine would simply sink her prey was unthinkable. Accordingly the value of the submarine as a commerce raiding weapon was dismissed since, to be effective, submarine commanders would have flagrantly to violate international law.

The early weeks of the First World War seemed to show that pre-war

---

[5]Rear-Admiral Sir William Jameson, *The Most Formidable Thing* (London: Hart Davis, 1965), pp.112–13.

doctrines about submarine operations were valid. The Germans employed their U-boats on defensive patrols in the Heligoland Bight while the Royal Navy used its submarines in the same waters to enforce the blockade of the High Seas Fleet. But on 20 October 1914 there occurred an event which was to have far-reaching consequences—the first sinking of a merchant ship by a U-boat. The 866grt *Glitra* was brought-to and sunk by *U17* (Feldkirchner) off Stavanger. Feldkirchner acted in accordance the Declaration of London and German Naval Prize Regulations but nevertheless was surprised when he was congratulated on his action rather than reprimanded—an indication of the attitudes prevailing within the German Navy.

It is difficult to say when the idea of using U-boats against British commerce first presented itself. The German official historian denies that any plans were made before the outbreak of the First World War to use U-boats in such a fashion. There is, however, evidence that the idea was given consideration, at least at an unofficial level. In such a study *Kapitänleutnant* Ulrich Blum, an officer on the staff of *Korvettenkapitän* Hermann Bauer, who was the head of the German Navy's submarine branch and who held the appointment of *Führer des U-bootes (FdU)*, had estimated that some 222 U-boats would be required for the successful blockade of the British Isles—a forecast that would prove to be remarkably accurate.

It was the early successes of the U-boats against British warships, such as the sinking of the British cruisers *Cressy*, *Hogue* and *Aboukir* on 22 September 1914 by *U9* (Weddigen), and patrol experience which showed *FdU* that U-boats could remain at sea for considerable periods. Accordingly Bauer submitted proposals for a commerce raiding campaign to *Admiral* von Ingenohl, commander-in-chief of the High Seas Fleet, in October 1914. Bauer stressed the uselessness of employing his U-boats in defensive patrols in the North Sea and concluded:

> A campaign of U-boats against commercial traffic on the British coasts will strike the enemy at his weakest spot and will make it evident both to him and to his allies that his power at sea is insufficient to protect his imports.[6]

---

[6] V. E. Tarrant, *The U-boat Offensive 1914–45* (London: Arms and Armour Press, 1989), p.12.

CHAPTER TWO

'An Altogether Barbarous Method of Warfare'

Our aim was to break the power of mighty England vested in her sea trade. —
Admiral Reinhard Scheer

I T WAS THE British blockade which provided the real stimulus for the campaign of unrestricted submarine warfare, despite the suggestions put forward for such a campaign from within the U-boat command before the war. Pre-war British policy placed a high value on the effects of economic pressure exerted on Germany. Although in 1914 the British Government announced that it would adhere to the terms of the Declaration of London, it then proceeded by means of Orders in Council issued on 21 September and 29 October 1914 to enlarge the lists of Absolute and Conditional Contrabrand by adding many of the commodities which had previously been declared Free.

The German offensive developed amid conflicting policies and was always beset by an inadequate number of U-boats to make the campaign effective. Initially the main argument in favour of the submarine offensive was that it was necessary to counter the effects of the British blockade. Those opposed to such a course argued that such a campaign would be bound to bring about the entry of the United States of America into the war on the side of the Entente powers. Each time the stranglehold on Germany's economy imposed by the British blockade pushed the German Government into declaring a campaign of unrestricted submarine warfare, fears that such an action would provoke the United States into entering the war would cause this decision to be revoked within a few months. It was not until the end of January 1917, when Germany's situation was indeed dire, that the Imperial Government decided that it had no option but to pursue the campaign to the bitter end, regardless of the consequences.

Thus the German campaign of unrestricted submarine warfare advanced in a series of leaps and bounds. Originally conceived as a short-term weapon aimed at mitigating the worst effects of the British blockade, it became the cornerstone of German strategy for winning the war once the High Command realized that victory on land could not be achieved. There were three distinct campaigns against Allied shipping before the final declaration of unrestricted submarine warfare in February 1917, the first from February to September 1915, the second from February to April 1916 and the third from October 1916 to January 1917.

In their campaign against British commerce, the Germans made use of cruisers, armed merchantmen (either converted liners operating as armed merchant cruisers or disguised ocean raiders) and U-boats. Though the cruisers and merchant raiders were moderately successful, notably the cruiser *Emden* in the Indian Ocean and the raider *Möwe* in the Atlantic, they were quickly rounded up and dispatched by the Royal Navy. It was the U-boats which bore the brunt of the offensive and which achieved the most successes.

Germany was the last of the great powers to commission submarines into her fleet—the first boat began her trials as late as 1907, by which time Britain, France and Italy all had sizeable numbers of submarines in commission. The late start, however, was not without its advantages. Germany was able to gain from the experience of the other powers in submarine development and at the outbreak of the Great War possessed a more modern fleet. The development of the German U-boat did not proceed evenly, however. The early boats, *U1* to *U18*, were fitted with Korting kerosene engines which left a distinctive exhaust trail that could be seen for miles by day, as could the sparks from the exhaust at night. It was not until *U19* was built that the more satisfactory MAN diesels were introduced. Nevertheless, there was a continual stream of development of bigger boats with enhanced endurance and armament which culminated in 1912 with the construction of the 'Thirties' class (*U31* to *U41*), which were an outstanding design for a nation that had spent only six years in the submarine construction business. The boats of the 'Thirties' class displaced 685/878 tons,[1] were armed with two bow and two stern 50cm (19.7in) torpedo tubes (six torpedoes were carried) and one 88mm KL/30 gun (later replaced with a 105mm KL/45 weapon) and were powered by two 1,850bhp MAN diesels and two 1,200shp motors, giving a maximum surfaced speed of 16.4kts and a maximum dived speed of 9.7kts. They were possessed of considerable qualities of endurance—7,800 nautical miles at 8kts.

The outbreak of war in August 1914 interrupted the otherwise smooth pace of German submarine development. At once the *Admiralstab* took steps to increase the size of the fleet by switching to a mobilization programme, the first boats—known as *Ms* boats—being *U51* to *U56*, which were merely improved versions of *U41*. However, it soon became apparent to the *Admiralstab* that these sophisticated submarines would take too long to build: something smaller and cheaper was required.

Immediately after the outbreak of hostilities the *U-Bootinspektion* was asked to prepare a study for a small, single-screw submarine which was simple to build and could be transported by rail in sections to the port of assembly. The concept was initially rejected but the swift conquest of the Belgian ports of Zeebrugge and Ostend brought new life to the project and

---

[1]Submarine tonnage is usually expressed as two figures. The first refers to displacement on the surface and the second to submerged displacement, the difference representing sea water taken on as ballast.

led to the development of a torpedo (*UB*) and minelayer (*UC*) type. In September 1914 the first of eighteen boats of the *UB1* group were ordered and the first prototype was built within a hundred days. *UB1* herself displaced 127/142 tons, was equipped with two 45cm bow torpedo tubes and was powered by a single Daimler four-cylinder, 60bhp diesel engine and a 120shp electric motor, giving a speed of 6.5/5.5kts. In October 1914 the first of fifteen *UC1* minelayers were ordered. Displacing only 168/183 tons, the *UC1* class were very functional craft, carrying no torpedo armament but instead twelve UC120 type mines in six free-flooding tubes in the hull forward of the conning tower. In both the *UB* and *UC* series, initial orders were deliberately kept low so that experience gained at sea could be incorporated into later programmes.

Thus by the spring of 1915 the German Navy possessed three types of submarine, each designed for different operations: the *U* boats came under the command of the Commander-in-Chief of the High Seas Fleet but could be released for commerce raiding in distant waters, while the *UB* and *UC* series boats came under the command of the newly established Flanders Flotilla (*Marinekorps U-Flotille Flandern*) for commerce raiding and mine-laying operations in the North Sea, English Channel and eastern areas of the Western Approaches. In time, when submarines were deployed to the Mediterranean, separate U-boat commands would be established at Pola (*Deutsche U-Halbflotille Pola*) and Constantinople (*U-Halbflotille Konstanti-nopel*), the former consisting of *U*, *UB* and *UC* types and the latter of *UB* and *UC* types only.

During the last months of 1914 and the early weeks of 1915 there was a lively debate within the German Government on whether or not to allow unrestricted submarine warfare, i.e. the sinking of merchant ships without warning. The protagonists said that it was the only way to deal with the threat posed by the English blockade, while the opponents claimed that the inevitable breaches of international law would result in conflict with the neutral states, particularly the United States. *Admiral* von Pohl, Chief of the Naval Staff, succeeded in convincing the faint-hearted that a campaign of unrestricted warfare would be successful. In order to minimize the diplomatic fall-out with the neutral states, a war zone was declared around the British Isles on 4 February 1915 in which all ships would be at risk, the zone to be effective from 18 February. The Germans justified this course of action by referring to British policy concerning the blockade but promised that every effort would be made save the crews of merchant ships. However, the announcement received a very hostile reaction in neutral countries and the Germans had to modify their original announcement by stating that those ships clearly identified as neutral would be spared.

The first campaign lasted for seven months, February to September 1915, but is best considered in two phases, January–May and June–September, the dividing point being the sinking of the *Lusitania* on 7 May 1915. When the

TABLE 1: MERCHANT SHIP LOSSES, MARCH–SEPTEMBER 1915[2]		
Month	**Ships lost**	**Tonnage**
March	29	89,517
April	33	41,448
May	53	126,895
June	114	115,291
July	86	98,005
August	107	182,772
September	58	136,408
Total	480	790,336

campaign began the Germans had 27 operational U-boats, 21 in the North Sea and available for commerce warfare and six in the Baltic. Another 75 were under construction. In the first three months of the campaign 38 out of 57 torpedo attacks were successful but four of the ships affected were able to make port. There were 93 attacks using gunfire, but 43 of these potential victims managed to escape, and 28 miscellaneous small craft were sunk (see Table 1).

These figures seem comparatively small and were easily matched by new construction. In the first quarter of 1915 only 267,000 tons of new merchant ships joined the fleet and this fell to 148,000 and 146,000 tons for the next two quarters respectively. The reason for the low construction rate for merchant shipping was that the yards were preoccupied with new warship construction and repair work. An additional factor was that 20 per cent of ocean-going tonnage had been taken up by the military for trooping and transport duties. The writing was on the wall for the British merchant marine but few saw it. However, the Exchange Rate was twenty merchant ships sunk for each U-boat sunk and there was very little that could be done about this.[3]

The turning point in the campaign was the sinking of the *Lusitania* by *U20* (Schweiger) on 7 May. The Cunard liner sank in twenty minutes with the loss of over 1,000 lives including those of American passengers. The rights and wrongs of Schweiger's attack have been endlessly debated and have no place here, but *Lusitania*'s sinking was to have severe diplomatic consequences for Germany. American opinion was outraged and Germany recognized this in June by prohibiting attacks on large liners. Nevertheless this restriction did not halt the offensive. This period was marked by a greater use of the gun (as opposed to the torpedo) by U-boat commanders. Not only was gun action more 'legal', but it was more efficient: more ships could be sunk by shellfire than by using the submarine's limited torpedo armament.

---

[2]These and other tonnage figures quoted in this chapter are from V. E. Tarrant, *The U-boat Offensive 1914–45* (London: Arms and Armour Press, 1989).

[3]Throughout this book reference is made to the Exchange Rate. This is a useful means of measuring the success or otherwise of a commerce raiding campaign. It is obtained by dividing the number of merchant ships sunk by the number of raiders lost. An Exchange Rate of more than 100 means that the campaign is doing spectacularly well, while one of 25 is about average; a rate of less than 10 means that the campaign is in deep trouble.

The principal area for U-boat operations was the Western Approaches. In June and July *U20* and *U39* sank twenty ships between them. In August no fewer than thirteen U-boats were at sea. *U38*, *U27* and *U24* all worked the Western Approaches, and shipping losses were higher than at any time in the war to that date. During the period of the first offensive the Germans lost fifteen U-boats, seven of them to Q-ships, but with over 100 boats under construction this loss rate could easily be sustained. In practical terms the first offensive had very little effect. Communications with France were not affected, neither were communications with the Entente forces in the Dardanelles; moreover, the neutral states trading with Britain had not been frightened off as the Germans expected they would be. The rate of loss was still only 1 per cent of the British merchant fleet, but by the end of the campaign the loss rate had risen above the rate of replacement.

The end to this promising campaign came suddenly on 19 August 1915 when the White Star liner *Arabic* was sunk by *U24* (Schneider). Once again there were Americans among the casualties and relations between Berlin and Washington became strained. At this stage in the war the moderates in German politics still had some influence and Chancellor Bethmann-Hollweg informed the outraged Americans that no further ships would be sunk without warning and that no passenger ships would be sunk at all. The Commander-in-Chief of the High Seas Fleet considered that these instructions were unduly restrictive and withdrew the boats under his command from commerce raiding, thereby effectively ending the offensive. The Flanders Flotilla boats followed suit and orders to cease the offensive on 18 September were issued.

American pressure had been the deciding factor in calling off the offensive, but in truth the High Seas Fleet boats were dangerously over-extended, many were in need of refit and only four could be maintained at sea. Another factor was the decision to send boats to the Mediterranean, where there were fewer targets which would cause complications with America and where there was a need to bolster Germany's ally, Turkey.

The Mediterranean was to be a particularly profitable theatre of operations for U-boats throughout the war. Three of the five top-scoring U-boat commanders, Arnauld de la Perrière, Max Valentiner and Walther Forstmann, earned their laurels in the Mediterranean. A flotilla of six *U* type boats plus nine *UB*s and *UC*s was maintained at Cattaro on the Adriatic and their successes formed a considerable proportion of the total amount of shipping lost to the U-boats: eighteen ships in September 1915, seventeen in October, 41 in November and 24 in December but only six in January 1916 because the boats were worn out and in need of refit. The majority of sinkings were made by gunfire, yet there were a number of attacks on troopships (quite legitimate targets), which were made without warning. Not one U-boat was lost in the Mediterranean despite the presence of 66 destroyers, 79 sloops and 200 trawlers—proof of the inadequacy of Allied ASW measures. Generally in the period October 1915 to February 1916, the interval between the first and second unrestricted offensives, 165 ships of 410,936 tons were lost.

The policy behind the construction of U-boats during the First World War was as haphazard as the development of the campaign they were to implement. When the first unrestricted campaign was declared on 1 February 1915, a further two dozen ocean-going *Ms* types were ordered (*U57–92*, less the five *UD* boats, *U66–70* requisitioned from Austria-Hungary and the ten *UE* type minelayers). These boats were merely upgraded versions of the *U27* or *U30* type. However, problems arose in that the diesel engines took longer to build than the boats themselves. At the same time it was realized that the small *UB* and *UC* types needed considerable modification since reports from sea indicated that these small boats, though fulfilling the role for which they were designed, were unequal to the new demands made by the unrestricted warfare campaign.

Accordingly the *UBII* and *UCII* classes made their appearance. The *UBII* type, first ordered in April 1915, was considerably larger than existing designs, at 263/292 tons displacement, and carried four (and later six) of the heavier 50cm torpedo, firing through two bow tubes. Twin Daimler, Korting or Benz diesels were fitted, giving a top speed of 9kts; two electric motors gave a top submerged speed of 5.8kts. The *UCII* type was also larger, at 417/480 tons, and possessed better sea-keeping and endurance (9,250nm at 8kts) qualities than its predecessors. The biggest difference, however, was in the armament: eighteen UC200 mines were carried in six mine wells with the addition of three 50cm torpedo tubes, two bow (external in some early boats) and one stern.

Yet no sooner had these boats been ordered and construction begun than their *raison d'être* was abandoned with the end of the first campaign of unrestricted submarine warfare. Construction was switched to large submarines suitable for commerce raiding under the Prize Rules (the two Project 43 boats which were never built) and the ten ocean-going minelaying boats of the *UE* type. Unlike its primitive forerunner, the *UE* was quite a sophisticated craft, carrying its 34 mines in dry stowage and armed with two 50cm torpedo tubes for active hunting. However, in March 1916, when the Germans once more reverted to unrestricted submarine warfare, they found themselves short of simple, mass-produced boats for torpedo warfare around the coasts of Britain. The resulting design was a compromise between the large and complicated *Ms* boats and the small and cheap *UBII* series boats. Known as the *UBIII* series, this represented a considerable increase in size on the *UBII*, at 516/651 tons displacement (which increased to 533/656 tons in later boats), with an increased armament of five 50cm torpedo tubes—four bow and one stern—with ten torpedoes carried. An 88mm gun, later replaced by a 10.5cm weapon, made up the surface armament. Though the *UBIIIs* were larger and faster than the *UBII* boats, the increase in armament was paid for by degraded speed and endurance compared with the *Ms* types.

Orders were placed for the first boats in May 1916 but problems in the shipyards meant that deliveries would not begin before the summer of 1917.

Throughout the winter of 1915–16 the debate raged in German political and military circles about the wisdom of continuing with a campaign of unrestricted submarine warfare. The blockade was having serious effects, particularly regarding the importation of nitrate fertilizers: although Germany was almost self-sufficient in food, this self-sufficieny depended on regular imports of nitrates to keep the predominantly sandy soil fertile, and without these imports on the soil would become impoverished, with devastating effects on cereal production for food and animal fodder. In short, Germany faced starvation on the home front while her armies remained undefeated in the field.

General Erich von Falkenhayn, the Chief of the General Staff, was confident that his forthcoming offensive at Verdun would break the stalemate on the Western Front and he saw a parallel offensive at sea breaking the Royal Navy. In this he was supported by *Admiral* Henning von Holtzendorff. Those in favour of a second unrestricted campaign were greatly assisted by an American Note issued in November 1915. The Americans conceded that a campaign against commerce was acceptable provided that neutral ships were not attacked and that crews were given the chance to leave the ship before she was sunk. The Americans went further and admitted that in order to escape attack merchant ships must not be armed, otherwise they could be treated as auxiliaries and sunk accordingly.

The second campaign developed amid considerable political muddle. The order was given to begin unrestricted warfare on 29 February 1916 but was quickly compromised by the instruction that large passenger ships were not to be attacked even if they were armed. On 4 March 1916 *Kaiser* Wilhelm II, the 'Supreme Warlord', gave his consent for a completely unrestricted campaign to begin on 1 April but lost his nerve when faced with the diplomatic consequences and withdrew his consent. As a result, *Admiral* von Tirpitz, the architect of the *Reichsmarine* and a supporter of unrestricted warfare, resigned.

The campaign was opened on 4 March 1916 by *U32*'s sinking of the 4,824-ton *Teutonian*. Spiedel, the U-boat's commander, allowed the crew to abandon ship before sinking her. However, the campaign was to be very brief—barely two months in all. In March 1916 the U-boats sank 69 ships grossing 169,536 tons and in April they sank 83 ships totalling 187,307 tons. Four U-boats were lost, *U68* to a Q-ship, *UB26* in nets off Le Havre, *UB17* mined and *UC5* run aground and captured, so the Exchange Rate was 38.

On 15 March the instructions were revised to state that all ships travelling in the War Zone could be sunk, except passenger ships—even if they were armed. This was more than Washington was prepared to accept. Matters came to a head with the sinking of the cross-channel steamer *Sussex* on 24 March by *UB29* (Pustkuchen). *Sussex* was carrying fifty Americans and a number of them were among the casualties. Pustkuchen claimed that the ship was carrying troops, but the Americans were not impressed:

> For the third time running the principle on which the Washington authorities stood firm was breached by a young fellow less than thirty years old, with nothing to guide him but his periscope and desire for professional distinction.[4]

On 24 April orders were issued for U-boats to operate solely in accordance with the Prize Rules. *Admiral* Reinhard Scheer, Commander-in-Chief of the High Seas Fleet, believed this to be both impractical and dangerous since it exposed his boats to the risk of being sunk by Q-ships, and he withdrew them from the commerce raiding campaign.

Short though it may have been, the second campaign convinced the *Admiralstab* that, with 38 new U-boats about to join the fleet, a monthly attrition rate against British merchant shipping of 160,000 tons was not impossible. The monthly rate of sinking was now almost twice the rate at which ships were being built, so the situation was becoming acute, particularly as the need for ships to support military operations overseas showed no signs of abating.

The period between the ending of the second offensive and the resumption of *Handelskrieg* (trade warfare) in October 1916 is known as the 'Twilight Period'. In home waters, U-boat operations were conducted mainly in support of the High Seas Fleet and proved singularly unsuccessful. However, the boats of the Flanders and Mediterranean Flotillas kept the average monthly loss at around 110 ships (see Table 2). During this period the boats in the Mediterranean were the most active. With only between three and five boats at sea at a time, they managed to sink 153 ships of 282,925 tons. Lothar von Arnauld de la Perrière of *U35* was the most prolific scorer. In three weeks he sank 54 ships of 91,000 tons using 900 rounds of 4in ammunition and only four torpedoes. In the Mediterranean the U-boats were helped by generally beneficial weather and the disjointed nature of the Allied ASW strategy.

With the abandonment of the second unrestricted warfare campaign in April 1916 the *Admiralstab* reverted to orders for large submarines fitted with a hefty gun armament for conducting commerce warfare according to the Prize Rules. Operational experience of handling these vessels had already been gained with the submarine cruiser *Deutschland*. Despite continuing delays in the production of diesel engines, the construction of the Project 46 and 46a boats (*U139–141*) went ahead. Room for these large vessels in the production programme was found by cancelling the *Ms* types *U111–114* and *U127–130*. The 'U-cruisers', as they were known, were very large submarines displacing 1,930/2,483 tons and armed with six 50cm torpedo tubes (two stern and four bow, for nineteen torpedoes carried) and two 15cm

---

[4]Tarrant, p.29.

TABLE 2: MERCHANT SHIP LOSSES, MAY–SEPTEMBER 1916

Month	Ships lost	Tonnage
May	63	119,381
June	63	93,193
July	95	110,928
August	113	163,145
September	172	231,573
Total	506	718,220

KL/45 guns. Two six-cylinder, four-stroke, 3,300bhp diesels gave a maximum surfaced speed of 15.3kts and an endurance of 12,630nm at 8kts. Two 1,690shp electric motors gave a top dived speed of 7.6kts and an endurance of 53nm at 4.5kts. A 450shp diesel generator was also fitted, to produce a burst of speed when required during an attack.

However, before these monster submarines could be launched the wheel had come full circle again and Germany had declared unrestricted submarine warfare for the third and final time. The U-cruisers were a design response to a type of warfare which had been made obsolescent and once again the need was for small, easily produced boats of the *UBIII* series. These boats had already been ordered in substantial numbers up to February 1917 (*UB88–132*) but were now ordered in greater numbers. In June 1917 U-boat production was accorded the highest priority and a further 95 boats were ordered, 37 *UBIII* types (*UB133–169*), nine *Ms* types (*U164–172*), ten U-cruisers (*U173–182*) and 39 *UCIII* types (*UC80–118*; the *UCIII* type was an upgraded version of the *UCII* minelayer). All these boats were scheduled for completion between the summer of 1918 and January 1919.

However, the German shipbuilding industry was finding it hard to meet the new production programmes. Workers were existing on an inadequate diet, thanks to the British blockade, and these problems were exacerbated by strikes, absenteeism and bad weather during the winter of 1917–18. The inept handling of the U-boat construction programme was the subject of some vehement criticism from the High Seas Fleet in December 1917 which resulted in a meeting between the *Reichsmarineamt* (Imperial Navy Office), the *Admiralstab* and the *Oberheresleitung* (Army High Command). Agreement was reached on the significance of the U-boat war within the context of Germany's overall strategy, but the Navy's plans to increase U-boat production by getting the Army to release labour and switch factories currently producing munitions to U-boat production were blocked by *General* Erich Ludendorff, the Principal Quartermaster General.

On 17 December 1917 the construction programme for 1919 was agreed. Despite all the problems in the shipyards and the fact that no extra resources would be released by the Army, the number of boats ordered, 120, was substantially above that approved for the 1918 programme. The 1919 programme consisted of 36 *UBIII* boats (*UB177–205*), 34 *UCIII* boats

(*UC119–152*), twelve *Ms* boats (*U201–212*), eighteen U-cruisers (*U183–200*) and twenty *UF* boats (*UF1–20*). The *UF* was a small (364/381 tons) boat with a relatively heavy armament of five 50cm tubes and an 88mm gun. It was designed for short-range, high-yield operations in the English Channel and its chief virtue was that it was a single-hull design: all the fuel tanks were inside the hull, which reduced the possibility of tell-tale leakages if the boat were depth-charged. This increased programme meant that eleven shipyards would now be working around the clock on nothing other than the building of U-boats. At this time the U-Boat Office was set up, largely at Scheer's instigation, to accelerate all aspects of U-boat production.

On 11 August 1918 *Admiral* Scheer became head of the *Admiralstab* and at once set about 'tightening up' U-boat production by means of the ambitious 'Scheer Programme', which called for an increase in production of one-third. Conference after conference was called to decide how to allocate the necessary steel, diesel engine production and manpower while the military situation around Germany gradually collapsed. The cessation of hostilities in November 1918 brought an end to this ambitious venture.

To return to the summer of 1916, following the Battle of Jutland *Admiral* Scheer submitted a confidential report to the *Kaiser* which summarized his views on naval strategy:

> There can be no doubt that even the most successful outcome of fleet action in this war will not force England to make peace. The disadvantages of our military-geographical position in relation to the British Isles, and the enemy's great material superiority, cannot be compensated for by our fleet to the extent where we shall be able to overcome the blockade or the British Isles themselves—not even if the U-boats are made fully available for purely naval operations. A victorious end to the war within a reasonable time can only be achieved through the defeat of British economic life—that is, by using U-boats against British trade. In this connection I feel it my duty to again strongly advise Your Majesty against the adoption of any half measures, not only because these would contradict the nature of the weapon and would produce commensurate results, but also because in British waters, where American interests are strong, it is impossible to avoid incidents, however conscientious our commanding officers may be: unless we can act with full determination such incidents involve us in the humiliation of having to give way.[5]

What Scheer was pressing for was the resumption of unrestricted warfare. The debate which rumbled on throughout the summer and autumn of 1916 was carried on against the background of the stalemate on the Western Front where Falkenhayn's much vaunted offensive against Verdun had got bogged down in a hideous and seemingly unending battle of attrition. Foreign Minister Gottlieb von Jagow was particularly unimpressed with the arguments for a resumption, stating that 'Germany will be treated like a mad

---

[5]A. Marder, *From the Dreadnought to Scapa Flow, Vol. 3: Jutland and Aftermath* (London: Oxford University Press, 1965), pp.253–4.

TABLE 3: MERCHANT SHIP LOSSES, OCTOBER 1916–JANUARY 1917

Month	Ships lost	Tonnage
October	185	341,363
November	180	366,689
December	197	307,847
January	195	328,391
Total	757	1,344,290

dog against which everybody will combine'.[6] Chancellor Bethmann Hollweg was in favour in theory but continually questioned the right time to put such a campaign into effect. By the end of September a tenuous form of agreement had been reached among all parties that an unrestricted campaign was a good idea. The qualifying factor was when such a campaign should begin.

As a compromise measure it was agreed that a campaign waged according to the Prize Rules should begin in October. Scheer, believing that approval for an unrestricted campaign would follow, released the High Seas Fleet boats for commerce raiding. At the beginning of October 1916 the Germans had 96 boats in commission in all theatres, 36 with the High Seas Fleet, 22 with the Flanders flotilla, 14 in the Baltic, 18 at Pola in the Mediterranean and six at Constantinople.

This 'restricted' campaign was very successful, average monthly sinkings running at twice those of August 1915, which had been the most successful month for the U-boats to date (see Table 3). Ten U-boats were lost during this period, compared with 757 merchant ships, making the Exchange Rate 75—a very satisfactory rate of sinkings.

By the beginning of 1917 the success of the restricted campaign was causing a revival of demands for a completely unrestricted one. With Rumania crushed and the British Somme and Russian Brusilov offensives contained, Germany's military position was now significantly better. Hindenburg and Ludendorff, who held the real power in the German Government, were completely in favour of an all-out offensive. In this they were supported by von Holtzendorff, who submitted a memorandum on 22 December 1917 claiming that within five months an all-out campaign would force England to make peace.

At a Crown Council at Pless on 9 January 1917 the matter was discussed but, in the face of the unwavering stance in favour of the unrestricted campagin by Hindenburg and Ludendorff, the *Kaiser* and the politicians swallowed their fears and agreed that the campaign should begin 'with the utmost severity' on 1 February 1917. What of the fear of America joining the Allied Powers which had so hamstrung the earlier offensives? This was contemptuously dismissed by Hindenburg and Ludendorff. They underestimated American determination and believed Holtzendorff's claim that

---

[6]Tarrant, p.34.

TABLE 4: MERCHANT SHIP LOSSES, FEBRUARY–MAY 1917		
Month	Tonnage lost	U-boats sunk
February	520,412	5
March	564,497	3
April	860,334	1
May	616,316	7
Total	2,561,559	16

Britain could be starved into submission before the Americans would be able to intervene effectively. Well might the German generals have echoed Field Marshal Haig's supposed prayer, 'Give us victory, before the Americans come'.

The demands of the military, backed up by the admirals and coupled with the *Kaiser*'s acquiescence and the abdication of responsibility by the politicians, had a common denominator—there really was no alternative but to declare unrestricted submarine warfare. The economic situation in Germany was desperate. The German armies in the field continued to be well fed and supplied, but this was at the expense of the civilian population, who were bearing the brunt of the effects of the blockade:

> The rations allowed were not always available. Many thousands of individuals could be sure of only five slices of bread, half a small cutlet, half a tumbler of milk, two thimblefuls of fat, a few potatoes and egg cup of sugar in the course of a day. To this the more fortunate could add a precarious, irregular supply of jams, green vegetables and nuts. These supplies were only obtainable by waiting for long hours in food queues, exposed to the rain, snow and slush of the bitter German winter: after obtaining them the women as often as not returned in their soaking clothes to houses that were not heated or even warmed . . . they were reduced to a condition which no community will endure indefinitely. The majority of the urban population were either cold or wet or hungry for the greater part of the day.[7]

The die was cast. The *Kaiser* ordered the campaign to begin on 1 February, an official announcement being made the day before in order to increase the psychological shock.

During the first three months of the campaign it seemed as if Holtzendorff's prediction would be realized. Although the average number of boats at sea in all theatres was only 36 (the maximum in any one day being 44), they took a terrific toll of British shipping, as indicated in Table 4.

Throughout the war the German Navy never had sufficient U-boats of the right type to make the campaign against Allied shipping effective. Construction was characterized by muddle and by reacting to events rather than building boats to implement a given policy. By the time U-boat production became really organized—with the mass ordering of the *UBIII* type in the summer of 1917—the full panoply of Allied countermeasures was deployed.

---

[7]A. C. Bell, *History of the Blockade of Germany and the Countries Associated with her in the Great War* (London: HMSO, 1961), p.601.

CHAPTER THREE

The Search for a Solution

It was at present a question of whether our armies could win the war before our navies lost it. — Colonel C. Repington, January 1917.

That celebrated phrase of Mahan's about Nelson's ghostly, unseen, storm-tossed fleet has been the Navy's undoing. — Lord Esher, British Envoy in Paris, May 1917.

H OW DID THE Royal Navy react to the onslaught on merchant shipping launched by the U-boats? True to pre-war thinking, it sought to protect trade by acting offensively. An astonishing variety of countermeasures were developed to deal with the U-boat—passive measures such as sophisticated minefields and barrages, combined with active measures like decoy vessels (better known as Q-ships), escorts armed with explosive sweeps or paravanes and later with depth charges, aircraft and submarines. The anti-submarine campaign absorbed a considerable amount of resources in terms of both manpower and *matériel*, yet by April 1917 only 48 U-boats had been sunk by enemy action. Moreover, the various anti-submarine measures had not the slightest effect on the continued onslaught on merchant shipping by the U-boats.

The sad truth was that in 1914 there was little that a warship could do when acting against a submarine. If the German *Admiralstab* had been slow to grasp the potential of the U-boat, then the British Admiralty had neither the means nor the tactics for dealing with a submarine. As Sir Henry Newbolt, the official historian of the war at sea in the Great War, later wrote, by the end of March 1917

> . . . there had been one hundred and forty-two actions between German submarines and British destroyers and the destroyers had only sunk their opponent in six of them. When therefore a German submarine commander fell in with a British destroyer, though perhaps he would have to submerge and chance his ground, still his chances of escaping destruction were about 23 to 1.[1]

Some of the ideas tried out in the early days of the war owed more to wishful thinking than to any serious analysis of the problem. Commander Kenneth Edwards recalled that the first anti-submarine patrol off Portland Harbour in 1914

> . . . was carried out by picket boats [small steam-boats]. Their anti-submarine armament consisted of a blacksmith's hammer and a canvas bag. The idea was

---

[1] V. E. Tarrant, *The U-boat Offensive 1914–45* (London: Arms and Armour Press, 1989), p.33, note 30.

that the hammer should be used to smash the periscope of the submarine, and the canvas bag to blind the submarine by being tied over the top of the periscope.[2]

The 'blinded' U-boat would then be forced to surface, where she would be sunk by gunfire. Other strange ideas included lance bombs for piercing the submarine's hull and training seagulls to perch on top of suitably exposed periscopes thus making them more visible. All these schemes, highly diverting though they appear, betrayed a fundamental lack of understanding of submarine warfare.

At the beginning of the war there was no one body within the Admiralty responsible for anti-submarine warfare. On 8 December 1914 the Submarine Attack Committee was formed, which would co-ordinate the development of anti-submarine measures until July 1915 when this work was taken over by the Board of Invention and Research. It would not be until 18 December 1916, when the Anti-Submarine Division was created at the Admiralty under Rear-Admiral Alexander A. L. Duff, that the campaign against the U-boat would be conducted on anything like professional lines.

Initially the Royal Navy placed its faith in passive measures designed to prevent the movement of U-boats to and from their bases, for example net barrages and minefields. In home waters, the Strait of Dover, the Heligoland Bight, the North Channel (between Ireland and the west coast of Scotland) and the area between the Orkneys and the Norwegian coast were all intensively mined. In the Mediterranean, the Strait of Otranto at the southern end of the Adriatic was likewise mined and barred with nets and drifters.

The Dover defences were the most crucial in view of the use made by the Germans of the ports of Ostend and Zeebrugge. The first minefields were laid from 2 October 1914 to 16 February 1915, when some 7,154 mines were placed to the east of the Strait. However, these fields were less than effective, on account of the miserable quality of the British mines. The latter were of two types, the 'Service' or naval spherical mine and the 'British Elia' mine which was based on an Italian design. Both would explode only when very violent contact was made with their firing arms. Other failings of the British mines were that they frequently sank, or were visible at low water, or drifted owing to the fact that their 8cwt sinkers were insufficient to keep them secure in the strong currents prevailing in the area.

The fields were supplemented by a force of drifters towing indicator nets made of a light steel mesh and fitted with a carbide flare which would ignite if the net were fouled by a submarine. Destroyers armed with explosive sweeps—80lb explosive charges each towed by two ships—supported the drifter patrol. By February 1915 thirty drifters towing nets were at work in the Strait of Dover, but although they accounted for the loss of *U8* (Stoss) on

---

[2] Lt-Cdr Kenneth Edwards, *We Dive at Dawn* (London: Rich & Cowan, 1939), p.369.

4 March 1915, they were very vulnerable to bad weather. The next stage in the blocking of the Dover Straits came in early 1915 when a plan for completely closing the channel by means of a heavy net supported by floating booms and secured to buoys running from Cap Gris Nez to Folkestone was considered. However, when by May 1915 little more than half the boom had been completed, the project was abandoned. Once again the weather was responsible: Vice-Admiral Reginald 'Porky' Bacon, commanding the Dover Patrol, wrote that 'It would be difficult for anyone who had not watched the behaviour of the boom in heavy weather to picture the strains and erosion to which the component parts of the structure were submitted.'[3]

In April 1916 the Dover defences were strengthened by the laying of 2,070 mines in a barrage of moored mine nets off the Belgian coast between Nieuport and the Scheldt estuary and supported by six deep fields of 4,862 mines, with the object of restricting the movement of the boats of the Flanders Flotilla to and from their bases at Ostend and Zeebrugge. However, the same defects with the mines persisted, rendering the new fields less than effective—*UB10* was actually ensnared in a mine net but escaped unscathed. The barrage was further extended in September 1916 with a line of indicator nets each studded with two electro-contact mines. The nets were suspended from buoys moored 500yds apart. The barrage stretched from the Goodwin Sands to the Snouw Bank off Dunkirk and was completed in October 1917. Because of the strong currents in the area the nets had to be shallow ones and thus were supported by three rows of deep mines laid to the west of the nets. At night the nets were illuminated by buoys fitted with flares. Although this represented a fairly comprehensive plan for denying the Channel to the U-boats, its effectiveness was compromised by a lack of supporting surface forces (unarmed drifters composed the majority of the back up) and because the weather played havoc with the nets. During the winter of 1916–17 it was estimated that only 25 per cent of the nets were effective. The mines were continually dragging and represented as great a menace to the ships of the patrols as they did to the U-boats. In the spring of 1917 the H-2 type mine was introduced into British service. This was a copy of a captured German mine, fitted with an improved firing circuit. Orders for 100,000 of this type were placed but by September 1917 only 1,500 had been produced.

By early 1918 it was recognized that the mine/net barrage laid across the Strait of Dover in 1916 was utterly ineffective in denying passage to the U-boats. In view of the gravity of the situation the Admiralty decided to replace Vice-Admiral Bacon with Vice-Admiral Roger Keyes, who had been Bacon's leading critic. Keyes assumed command of the Dover forces on 1 January 1918 and at once set about pursuing a more active policy. The mine/net barrage was abandoned (the buoys and nets were not replaced when they broke adrift) and instead it was decided to close the Strait by laying a vertical,

---

[3]Admiral Sir Reginald Bacon, *From 1900 Onward* (London: Hutchinson, 1940), p.255.

deep-mine barrage of parallel fields, using the new H-2 mine, from Folkestone to Cap Gris Nez at depths of between 30ft and 100ft below low water. Keyes used the craft formerly employed in maintaining the nets to conduct massed patrols of the minefields, with between eighty and a hundred vessels on station during the day. In order to ensure that U-boats did not slip through the Strait on the surface at night, the area above the barrage was to be brilliantly illuminated using searchlights and burning flares. The work was completed in February 1917 and continually updated so that by the end of the war 9,573 mines had been laid in twenty main parallel lines covering an area six miles wide, broken in two places by 'gates' for shipping.

Yet, for all the work that went into laying and patrolling these barrages, they proved to be singularly ineffective against the U-boats. The poor quality of the mines used was one factor, as was the lack of surface assets to ensure that the nets and mines were adequately patrolled. In 1917 the Admiralty estimated that as many as thirty U-boats a month were transiting the Strait of Dover, either by sneaking through on the surface at night or by diving through the minefields by day. The situation in the other barrages was little different. *Kapitänleutnant* Max Valentiner, commanding officer of *U33* and one of Germany's U-boat 'aces' of the Great War, summed up the situation in the Strait of Otranto perfectly: 'The attempt to block completely a piece of water 40 miles across is condemned to failure at the outset'. The fixed barrages were also vulnerable to attack by German or Austro-Hungarian surface forces. On 15 May 1917 the light cruisers *Novarra*, *Saida* and *Helgoland* raided the Otranto Barrage, sinking fourteen of the forty-seven drifters on patrol and damaging a further four. As a result of this raid the drifters were recalled to harbour at night, thus making a nonsense of the whole proceedings. A similar raid by German destroyers on the Dover Barrage on the night of 14–15 February 1918 resulted in eight drifters being sunk and a further six craft damaged.

Though generally agreed to be useless, the fixed barrages did exercise a limited effect on the conduct of U-boat operations. In early 1915, after *U33*, *U35* and *U28* had reported seeing nets and minefields (and in *U35*'s case being snared by a mine cable), *FdU* forbade his boats from using the Strait as a route to their operational areas in the Western Approaches. This was a serious tactical restraint since it added nearly 1,400 miles to a U-boat's journey and reduced the time she could spend in her operational area. The restriction remained in force until December 1916, although the Admiralty did not appreciate its significance. As the Dover defences were constantly improved, the number of U-boat commanders coming back from patrol with hair-raising tales of being caught in nets or minefields increased. In February 1917 passage of the Strait, which had been made compulsory in January 1917, was once again made optional, but this decision was overturned on 1 November 1917 when the new *FdU*, *Kapitän zur See* Andreas Michelsen (who had also assumed the title *Befehlshaber der U-boote*), ordered the boats

1. Admiral Sir John ('Jacky') Fisher, who saw the inevitability of unrestricted submarine warfare.

▲2

▲3 ▼4

2. *U6*, *U7* and *U8* manoeuvring at Kiel before the war.

3. *U17*, which opened the German commerce-raiding campaign when she sank the *Glitra* on 20 October 1914.

4. *U20* was one of the earliest diesel-engine boats in the German Navy. She sank the *Lusitania* on 7 May 1915.

5. The graves of some of those drowned when the *Lusitania* went down in May 1915. The sinking of the Cunard liner was a turning point in the first campaign against commerce.

6. *Korvettenkapitän* Hermann Bauer, the first *FdU* and a firm supporter of unrestricted submarine warfare.

7. *Admiral* von Pohl, Chief of the German Naval Staff, who, after some hesitation, became an advocate of the unrestricted campaign.
8. *UC1*, the first of the *UC* class of submarine minelayers which were to prove such a nuisance in the waters around Britain's East Coast.

▲7   ▼8

9. Loading a moored mine into a *UCII* class minelayer at Zeebrugge. Eighteen mines were carried in six shafts which sloped gently towards the stern.

10. Inside the engine room of an unidentified U-boat. The interior of such boats was cramped, noisy and smelly.

9▲   10▼

2746

▲11

▲12   ▼13

11. *U117*, an ocean-going *UE* class minelayer.

12. *UC72*, a *UCIII* class minelayer. The demands of the unrestricted campaign called for more and more boats of the small *UB* and *UC* types.

13. *UB122* was a *UBIII* type boat designed for unrestricted submarine warfare but she sank only one ship in her career.

14. *U86*, an ocean-going boat of the High Seas Fleet.

15. Lothar von Arnauld de la Perrière, commanding officer of *U35*, which sank 194 ships totalling 453,716 tons.

▲16   ▼17

16. Commerce-raiding according to the rules: the U-cruiser *U157* holds up the Spanish liner *Infanta Isabel de Bourbon* on 28 March 1918.

17. *Generale* Hindenburg (left) and Ludendorff (right), the real power brokers in Germany, who turned to unrestricted submarine warfare as a means of breaking the deadlock on land.

18. U-boat officers on the garlanded bridge of their submarine before going out on patrol, April 1917. They had every expectation that victory lay within their grasp.

19. The lance bomb was an imaginative but unpractical early means of dealing with a U-boat.

▲ 20

20. Barrage vessels at Dover equipped with searchlights for night operations.

21. Motor launches in the Eastern Docks at Dover. The various barrages tied up considerable numbers of forces.

22. Drifters at Taranto for service with the singularly ineffective Otranto Barrage.

23. Mines awaiting dispatch from the huge mine depot at Grangemouth in Scotland. Considerable faith was placed in mine barrages.

▼ 21

22▲   23▼

▲24

▲25　▼26

24. HMS *Lily* at Malta in 1917. *Lily* was an *Acacia* class sloop built in 1915, of 1,200 tons displacement, 250ft long and armed with two 12pdrs and two 3pdrs, together with an outfit of depth charges.

25. HMS *Poppy*, an *Arabis* class sloop, slightly larger than the *Acacia*s and carrying an increased armament of two 4.7in guns.

26. HMS *P48*, described as a 'utility destroyer'. Though possessed of dubious sea-keeping qualities, these useful ships were armed with one 4in gun, one 2pdr and two 14in torpedo tubes. Nearly all the class were assigned to the Dover Barrage force.

27. HMS *Kilmalcolm*, a 'Kil' class patrol vessel designed with an identical fore and aft silhouette to confuse an attacking submarine. Although their armament comprised just one 4in gun plus depth charges, these vessels had considerable qualities of endurance.

28. *Baralong*, a Q-ship which on 19 August 1915 disposed of *U27* in circumstances which are still a matter of controversy.

29. A 3in bomb thrower, a common weapon on board Q-ships. There is no record of it being used successfully.
30. HM submarine *R7*, one of eight 'R' class boats built specially for anti-submarine operations. Their streamlined hull, sophisticated asdic suite and heavy armament of six 18in torpedo tubes, all in the bow, gave them capabilities well in advance of their time.
31. A Short Type 184 seaplane taxiing prior to an anti-submarine patrol in 1918.
32. Using a hydrophone from a drifter on the Otranto Barrage. The Chief Petty Officer is 'listening' while a rating prepares to lower another microphone.

▲29   ▼30

▲33

33. Depth charges secured to the stern of a destroyer, April 1918.

34. Survivors from a sunken merchant ship come ashore at a British port in 1917. Such scenes became all too common as the German campaign got under way.

▼34

to use the Strait. However, by February 1918 Michelsen was forced to leave the decision on whether to go 'north about' or use the Strait of Dover to the discretion of individual commanding officers. The massed patrols, minefields and net barrages of the Dover defences had accounted for 28 U-boats but the other barrages for a far fewer number.

The doctrine of 'seek and destroy the enemy' governed more active operations against the U-boats. The Admiralty possessed a considerable number of operational resources in this campaign, including destroyers, the ships of the Auxiliary Patrol, decoys or Q-ships, submarines and aircraft. Early in the war the Admiralty had concluded that the destroyer, with its good sea-keeping qualities and gun armament, was the ideal anti-submarine weapon. By January 1916 thirteen destroyer leaders and 127 destroyers had been ordered.

However, in practice the destroyers were less than successful as submarine hunters. Used in this role they can best described as sprinters selected to run a long-distance race. Their high-performance machinery—a British 'M' class destroyer had a top speed of between 34 and 36kts—was intended for operations with the Fleet, where short, sharp engagements with the opposition's destroyer flotillas would be their likely *modus operandi*. The operations which destroyers were now required to undertake called for qualities of endurance and stamina rather than short-term performance. Moreover, destroyers were complex ships to build, each taking, on average, eighteen months to complete. As the shipbuilding capacity was already taken up with repair work and other warship construction, the destroyer programme ran into difficulties and the building time lengthened. Once commissioned the ships were often allocated to the Grand Fleet—which required around eighty such ships to provide an adequate destroyer screen—or the Mediterranean theatre, or to covering individual ship or squadron movements. There were never enough to go around, but at the beginning of the war they were all that existed.

The Auxiliary Patrol, instituted in the first days of the war, was composed of small yachts, trawlers and motor boats crewed by officers and men from the reserves. By the end of 1914 there were 750 vessels employed in the Patrol, a number which would rise to 3,100 by the end of the war. The standard unit consisted of a yacht, four trawlers and four motor boats. Eventually the ships of the Patrol were deployed into twenty areas which supposedly provided a protective belt around the British coast. In practice, however, the Auxiliary Patrol's effects were moral rather than actual. One authority went so far as to state that 'I don't think they did much except enhearten us by being busy'.[4]

The requisitioned ships of the Auxiliary Patrol were soon supplemented by

---

[4]A. Marder, *From the Dreadnought to Scapa Flow, Vol. 2: The War Years to the Eve of Jutland* (London: Oxford University Press, 1965), p.357.

large numbers of small, newly constructed ships—the so-called 'Mosquito Fleet' of sloops, P-boats, Admiralty-designed trawlers and drifters. When Arthur Balfour succeeded Winston Churchill as First Lord of the Admiralty in May 1915, the efforts to build up a large number of small craft were intensified. One of Balfour's first decisions was to order 36 sloops, and these would be supplemented later in the year with further vessels.

The Auxiliary Patrol first began operations on the basis of following up each reported U-boat 'incident'—a classic example of bolting the stable door after the horse had gone. Unfortunately there was so much water to be covered that encounters between these mixed forces and an enemy submarine could be hardly anything other than accidental. From 1915 a policy of tactically routeing merchant shipping away from areas where a U-boat was known to be operating was followed. However, behind this 'Dispersed Routeing' policy lay the grim facts of geography: shipping seeking entry to British ports had to follow one of three routes, towards Liverpool, Bristol or Southampton. Ships proceeding to Britain were dispersed in mid-ocean but gradually came together as they neared what one authority[5] has called the 'four great cones of approach', being drawn into conspicuous and vulnerable flocks as the 'cones' narrowed. The four 'cones' were defined as follows:

1. From the Mediterranean and South Atlantic, making for Bristol and the Channel Ports and converging on the Scilly Isles;

2. From the Caribbean and South America, heading for Bristol and Liverpool and converging at Fastnet Rock;

3. From North America and Canada, making for Liverpool and the Clyde and converging on Tory Island; and

4. From North America and Canada, making for East Coast ports by the 'north-about' route and converging on the Orkneys.

Within these areas the patrols would operate intensively, looking for submarines. In practice, however, the mere presence of the patrols indicated trade routes to the U-boat commander, who would quietly wait for the patrol to pass before 'rolling up' the shipping. Lloyd George was more direct in his criticism of Dispersed Routing: 'By this egregious method, the ships were often shepherded into the abattoir where the slaughterers lay in wait'.[6]

The *ad hoc* system of patrols was regularized in July 1915 with the establishment of a central command for anti-submarine operations. The impetus for this move came from Admiral Sir John Jelicoe, Commander-in-Chief of the Grand Fleet, who was alarmed at the fact that the first U-boat campaign against shipping was meeting with success while continuing to pose a threat to the Fleet. In June 1915 Jellicoe had written to Balfour advocating the appointment of a 'capable officer' whose job it would be to

[5] J. Terraine, *Business in Great Waters: The U-boat Wars 1916–45* (London: Leo Cooper, 1989), p.41.

[6] J. Winton, *Convoy: The Defence of Sea Trade 1890–1990* (London: Michael Joseph, 1983), p.49.

. . . watch submarines that are located, and to get all available craft on to them on their probable course. There is much valuable information daily at the Admiralty on the subject. A close study of this information enables one to judge the course and speed of certain submarines and predict the times they will pass through certain areas.[7]

Jellicoe was supported in this argument by Vice-Admiral Sir David Beatty, commanding the battlecruisers of the Grand Fleet. However, it must be stressed that both these flag officers' principal concerns lay with protecting the battle-fleet rather than curbing the U-boats' attacks on merchant ships.

On 25 July 1915 Admiral Sir Lewis 'Luigi' Bayley hoisted his flag at Queenstown (now Cóbh) as Admiral Commanding the Western Approaches (the title changed in May 1916 to Commander-in-Chief of the Western Approaches). Bayley's remit covered all the Western Approaches to the British Isles, including the Irish coasts, St George's Channel, the Bristol Channel and the entrance to the English Channel. To cover this area Bayley was provided with over 450 ships—destroyers, sloops, trawlers and a submarine. The trawlers worked off the coasts hunting for submarines or escorting individual ships, the drifters operated indicator nets in areas which it was important to keep clear, squadrons of eight sloops patrolled specified areas on the trade route south of Ireland while the submarines—only one was at sea at a time—operated off the south-west coast of Ireland. It was an ingenious and comprehensive scheme which owed much to Bayley's energy and to his no-nonsense attitude to his command, yet it was singularly ineffective. The U-boats generally operated well outside the range of the patrols—eighty miles offshore—where they could find all the targets they wanted.

Patrolling was not the answer to the U-boat problem, no matter how numerous the patrolling craft became:

It was extremely rare for patrols to be in the right place at the right time in the right force to repel an attack on a merchant ship, still less to find the enemy before he has attacked.[8]

Patrolling became a series of futile follow-up operations after U-boats had achieved successful attacks in a diversity of places. The one place where a U-boat could be guaranteed *not* to be found was where it had just left a 'flaming datum' in the water. The hunting of submarines by the patrols was a waste of time and resources except where luck intervened on the patrols' side or the U-boat commander made a mess of things. Yet the only complaint was that patrolling was not carried out as efficiently as it ought to be. 'Strategically, our pundits at the Admiralty have not yet realized that the way to protect

---

[7] Jellicoe to Beatty, 18 June 1915. British Museum, London: Balfour MSS.

[8] Marder, p.358.

trade is to cruise constantly in certain areas through which the trade passes,' wrote Captain Herbert Richmond in 1916.[9]

A variant on the patrolling system was the sweep by destroyers and submarines detached from the Grand Fleet. Such an operation carried out in June 1917 involved four destroyer leaders, fifty destroyers and seventeen submarines. The plan was for the force to sweep down the North Sea from the north-west, looking for U-boats going on or returning from patrol via the 'north-about' route. Destroyers and submarines would be disposed in adjacent patrol areas and the idea was that the destroyers would force the U-boats to dive and keep them down, depleting their batteries until the boats would have to surface, whereupon they would be torpedoed by one of the submarines. The scheme was a complete failure: there were 61 sightings of submarines and twelve attacks, but no sinkings. Yet during the sweep ten U-boats successfully transited the area without interference. The reaction of the Admiralty to this dismal performance was that the experiment 'ought to be repeated to give it a fair trial'.[10]

'Special service vessels', or Q-ships as they were popularly known, were another weapon in the Admiralty's armoury and were a trick as old as naval history. Beginning in November 1914, the Admiralty prepared a number of decoy vessels disguised to look like innocuous tramp steamers or sailing vessels but carrying a formidable gun armament, 6pdrs or 12pdrs in the earlier ships although later vessels carried the heavier 4in or 4.7in guns. These ships would cruise the trade routes hoping to entice a U-boat to the surface where it would be dispatched by gunfire and given the *coup de grâce* with a depth charge (when these weapons became available). They achieved their first success on 24 July 1915 when *U36* (Graeff) was sunk by the decoy ship *Prince Charles* north of Scotland. Over 180 such Q-ships were fitted out, but they only accounted for eleven U-boats—7 per cent of the total known to have been sunk—against a loss of 27 Q-ships. Seven of that number were sunk before the declaration of unrestricted submarine warfare, the remainder after that date, when the Q-ships were employed as convoy escorts.

In a sense Q-ships were a self-defeating weapon in that they precipitated an escalation of the conflict. Once news of their activities became widespread—particularly after the notorious sinking of *U27* by the Q-ship *Baralong* on 19 August 1916, in which the U-boat's commanding officer, *Kapitänleutnant* Bernhard Wegener, and about a dozen of his crew were shot after abandoning their submarine—U-boat commanders were wary of approaching individual merchant ships and would sink first and ask questions later. In any case, with the declaration of full unrestricted submarine warfare in 1917, the U-boats would simply sink on sight. An interesting variant on the decoy theme was the submarine trap. Following the depredations among the North Sea fishing

---

[9]*Ibid.*

[10]Winton, p.71.

fleet made by U-boats in 1915, it was suggested that a submarine should be towed, submerged, by a trawler, the two linked together by a telephone cable. The scheme worked: on 23 June 1915 *C24* torpedoed *U40*, while on 20 July 1915 *C27* torpedoed *U23*. Against these successes must be placed the loss of *C29*, which was accidentally towed into a minefield off the Humber on 29 August 1915. The scheme was finally abandoned in November 1915 when the crew of *U23*, repatriated to Germany, told of how their submarine had been sunk.

Submarines were also employed in a U-boat hunting role and accounted for fifteen of them, all in home waters except for *UB52*, sunk by *H4* on 25 May 1918 in the Adriatic. These submarine patrols were either in support of the various barrage forces (*H4* was operating in support of the Otranto Barrage forces) or in specially allocated patrol areas. The patrols were not without their perils, for the submarine is no man's friend and was in as much danger from her own side as she was from the enemy. *G9* was rammed in error by the destroyer HMS *Pasley* in the North Sea on 16 September 1917, *D3* was bombed in error by a French airship off Fécamp on 13 March 1918 and *J6* was sunk in error by the Q-ship *Cymric* on 15 October 1918.

An unusual development in the use of submarines as U-boat hunters was the construction of the eight 'R' class submarines, whose streamlined hulls gave them a submerged speed of 15.5kts against a surfaced speed of 9.5kts. They possessed a very complex hydrophone array and carried the heaviest torpedo armament (six 18in bow tubes) of any British submarine except *K26*. *R8* was the only one of the class to engage a U-boat: in an attack in October 1918 she fired at a U-boat but the torpedo did not run straight.

Air power in the shape of seaplanes and airships was the final asset available to the Admiralty in the war against the U-boat. However, the serious use of these machines against U-boats did not commence until the formation of the Anti Submarine Division at the Admiralty in December 1916. Although aircraft did not score any successes until well into 1917, their use will be considered here since it exemplifies the Admiralty's belief that the best way to protect trade was to go after the U-boat. Initially they were employed in the North Sea, Admiral Bayley at Queenstown being less than enthusiastic about their capabilities. Intelligence gleaned from decoded German wireless signals indicated that U-boats heading for the East Coast would take bearings from the North Hinder lightvessel. Accordingly, a patrol of flying boats worked a 'Spider Web' patrol off that lightvessel which began on 13 April 1917 and covered an area of 4,000 square miles. Over the next seventeen days 27 patrols were made, during which eight U-boats were sighted and three of these bombed. Minelaying off Harwich eased off and on 20 May 1917 *UC36* was sunk. Kite balloons towed by destroyers were another aspect of the 'air power' used against the U-boat: on 12 July 1917 a kite balloon towed by HMS *Patriot* sighted *U69*, which was eventually sunk by depth charge.

However, the sinking of *U69* demonstrated a problem which faced all the assets which Admiralty was able to deploy against the U-boat: as *Patriot* was steaming towards the U-boat at 25kts with her guns' crews closed up, *U69* dived and was lost to sight. Had not the U-boat lost her trim and inadvertently surfaced again, giving away her position, she might well have got away. The fundamental problem confronting the U-boat hunters was, how could you attack an enemy you could neither see nor track unless he gave away his position?

Finding and attacking the U-boat were the problem. German wireless traffic gave a good indication of how many boats were at sea and their rough locations. From the beginning of the war, the Royal Navy, through the activities of Room 40 at the Admiralty, was able to read German signal traffic. In this it was aided by the fact that the German Navy possessed superb wireless equipment: for example, its main transmitter at Nauen, near Berlin, could be heard as far afield as America and South-West Africa, and U-boats could communicate with their bases from distances as great as 800 miles. This unexpected attribute contained a built-in hazard—German submarine commanders were too free in using their wirelesses. Thus, with the help of the French DF Service, the Admiralty had a good general picture of U-boat operations, although the problems of localizing specific boats and attacking them remained.

The hydrophone, enabling the U-boat to be detected by the sound emanating from her motors, proved to be answer to the problems. Devised in 1915 by Professor William Bragg of Cambridge University and perfected by Commander C. P. Ryan RN, the hydrophone evolved into two types, directional and non-directional. Non-directional hydrophones simply picked up noise, whereas the directional type were more sophisticated and could be used to determine the bearing of the target. A further refinement came with the development of the 'fish' hydrophone, which could be towed outboard of a vessel, thus reducing interference from the latter's own machinery. Hydrophones were distributed for training purposes in April 1917 and by December that year 3,680 non-directional hydrophones had been distributed together with 1,950 Mks 1 and 2 directional hydrophones. The advances in hydrophone technology during the First World War were impressive and by the end of the conflict submarine hunts of up to thirty hours' duration were taking place.

But there remained the problem of how to attack a submerged submarine once she had been located. The early weapons consisted of the explosive sweep and then the paravane. The sweep had been developed by the pre-war Submarine Attack Committee and consisted of an 80lb charge towed by a plain (i.e. non-serrated) wire sweep from two ships. A modified version consisted of nine 80lb charges linked together and fired electrically from the towing vessel. Sweeps accounted for but one submarine, *U8*, which had already advertised her location by becoming entangled in a net. The paravane which was developed from the sweep in late 1915 was more effective and consisted of a 400lb charge which could be towed by a destroyer at speed. However, both the sweep and the paravane suffered from the same problem: towing them severely handicapped the ship's freedom to manoeuvre and there was always the risk of getting the wire wrapped around a propeller. The real answer lay in the development of the depth charge.

The antecedents of the depth charge go back further than one might suppose. It was 1914 when Admiral Sir George Callaghan, Jellicoe's predecessor as Commander-in-Chief of the Grand Fleet, requested some 'dropping mines' following an idea put forward in 1911. It was not until 1916 that a satisfactory 'dropping charge' or 'depth charge' became available—the Type D, with a charge of 300lb of TNT. A modified type, the Type D* with a lesser charge of 120lb, had to be issued to vessels smaller and slower than destroyers to protect them from the shock of the explosion (although the introduction of a variable-depth hydrostatic pistol with settings of 100, 150 and 200ft rendered the Type D* unnecessary). Delays in production meant that this weapon did not reach the ships of the Fleet as quickly as it might have done. In early 1917 ships could only take two Type Ds and two Type D*s to sea with them and it would not be until 1918 that a ship could take a full outfit of thirty-five charges to sea.

With the depth charge came the problem of delivery. Initially it was sufficient to roll the weapon over the stern but it soon became apparent that better results could be achieved by delivering multiple numbers of depth charges in patterns around the ship. Accordingly, depth-charge throwers were developed which could eject a charge out to a range of 40yds from the ship. By the end of the war an idea was developing which would not come to fall fruition until the next world war—the ahead-throwing weapon. Some 377 of these howitzers, which had a range of 1,200–2,600yds ahead of the ship, had been issued by the end of the war, although the small bursting charge of the projectile meant that a direct hit was essential. The first sinking of a U-boat by depth charge came on 22 March 1916 when the Q-ship *Farnborough* sank *U68* off the coast of Kerry, Ireland.

It was thus with these resources—destroyers, newly built escorts, hurriedly reconditioned vessels and fleets of trawlers, warned by radio intercepts and D/F bearings, hoping for precise detection by hydrophone and armed with depth charges—that the Navy applied itself to the task of hunting the U-boat. Despite the effort and expenditure, however, there was little to show for it all by way of results. By the end of January 1917 a total of forty-eight U-boats had been sunk. The breakdown of these losses according to cause is as follows:

Explosive sweep	1	Mine	4
High-speed paravane	1	Destroyer depth charge	1
Q-ship gunfire	5	Indicator nets	1
Q-ship depth charge	1	Rammed by warship	5

| Torpedoed by submarine | 5 | Accident | 7 |
| Gunfire of small craft | 3 | Unknown | 14 |

It was hardly auspicious. American protests at the activities of U-boat commanders had a greater effect in curbing the U-boats' activities than did the whole panoply of measures thrown up by the Admiralty.

Throughout this catalogue of the development of anti-U-boat measures the word 'convoy' has not been mentioned and the omission is deliberate. Convoy was seen as a 'defensive' measure whereas the Admiralty's policy was governed by the dogma of 'Seek out and destroy the enemy', which, as Professor Arthur Marder has pointed out, 'governed all activities and precluded rational thought'.[11] By concentrating on hunting the submarine, the Admiralty were ignoring the fact that U-boat activities were turning the Western Approaches into a graveyard for Britain's merchant marine. Something had to be done or Britain would lose the war. The 'something' would be the introduction of the convoy system which concentrated all these strands of anti-submarine warfare—ships, aircraft, hydrophones and depth charges—where they would be most effective. However, it would take a crisis in the war before convoy was introduced. How that crisis occurred is the subject of the next chapter.

---

[11]Marder, p.367.

CHAPTER FOUR

1917: The Anvil of Victory

The system of several ships sailing together in a convoy is not recommended in any area where submarine attack is a possibility. — Admiralty Staff Paper, January 1917

A T THE TIME of the writing of the Staff Paper from which the quotation heading this chapter was taken, German U-boats operating in Home Waters and the Mediterranean had sunk 368,521grt of Entente merchant shipping. The employment of considerable anti-submarine forces and development of new weapons had not, in the words of Professor Marder, 'caused the German submarine commanders to alter their tactics or procedure in any important particular'.[1] Shipping losses would rise until April 1917, when the total sunk registered tonnage sunk was 860,354. Yet throughout the first five months of 1917, while shipping losses steadily mounted as the German campaign of unrestricted submarine warfare began to bite, the Admiralty steadfastly maintained their opposition to convoy as a means of protecting trade. All the Admiralty could offer was more of the same: more patrolling, increased mining of German U-boat bases and the tactical routeing of shipping away from known U-boat operating areas.

The Admiralty's arguments against convoy were partly strategic in nature, partly tactical and partly a result of complacency brought about by an inadequate statistical analysis of British merchant shipping movements. Strategically speaking, the Admiralty misunderstood its objective. It was considered that the best way of protecting trade was to proceed directly against the threat (the U-boat), leaving the victims (the merchant ships) pretty much to their own devices. Their Lordships failed to understand that their objective was to ensure the safe arrival and departure of merchant ships loaded with the food and supplies on which Britain's survival depended. It mattered not, therefore, *how many* U-boats were at sea so long as the merchant ships were proceeding unmolested. The cause of this misunderstanding lay in the belief that convoy was defensive whereas charging all over the ocean in the fruitless search for a periscope was offensive. To the Royal Navy officer of 1917, offensive action was infinitely preferable to defensive action.

The Royal Navy mustered a whole host of tactical arguments against

---

[1]Quoted in J. Terraine, *Business in Great Waters: The U-boat Wars 1916-45* (London: Leo Cooper, 1989), p.86.

convoy, described by one author as akin to a 'hydra'.[2] One of the main objections was that a convoy would simply provide the U-boat with a larger target—a self-defeating argument since the opposite point of view, that convoy offered merchant ships greater protection through concentration of force, was not considered. However, most of the opposition merely reflected quite unjustified prejudice against the professional competence of the Merchant Navy—for example, merchant ships would find it impossible to manoeuvre together in convoy and they would straggle at night. It was also argued that the arrival of a convoy would place an intolerable strain on port facilities and lead to shipping being needlessly delayed while waiting to load or discharge cargo. Lastly, convoy would prevent fast merchant ships from using their speed as a means of defence.

The apparent complacency with which the Royal Navy viewed the decimation of Britain's merchant marine was bolstered by an inadequate statistical knowledge of what was going on. In March 1917 the Admiralty estimated that there were approximately 5,000 weekly shipping movements to and from British ports. This improbable figure meant that some 200 million tons of goods were being imported every year—six times the pre-war annual level! Commander R. G. Henderson, of the Anti Submarine Division, discovered that these figures could not be substantiated and, with the assistance of Norman Leslie of the Ministry of Shipping, undertook a survey of Britain's maritime trade. He discovered that the situation was very much worse. There were roughly twenty arrivals and twenty sailings from British ports each day—a far lower level of activity than was previously thought. Moreover, Henderson discovered that by the end of April 1917 there were 3,200 merchant ships in British service, or approximately 5 million tons of shipping. Of this figure, 1,900 ships were required for war work, leaving 1,300 for carrying the food and raw materials on which the war effort depended. At the time, ten ships a day were being sunk: one merchant ship in four leaving the country was failing to return. With such erroneous figures as their only evidence, the Admiralty's complacency is understandable: to lose 50 ships out of 5,000 shipping movements is one thing, but to lose 50 ships out of 120 movements is a disaster.

The introduction of convoy in May 1917 is often represented, usually by those with an axe to grind, as a victory for the clever politicians over a reactionary and hidebound Admiralty:

> At dead of night, Lloyd George consulted junior naval officers. He accumulated figures and arguments. On 26 April, he went to the Admiralty, armed with his authority as Prime Minister and the backing of the War Cabinet. He took his seat at the head of the Admiralty Board. He gave the formal order that convoys must be instituted. The admirals belatedly discovered that they had been in favour of convoys all along.[3]

---

[2] J. Winton, *Convoy: The Defence of Sea Trade 1890–1990* (London: Michael Joseph, 1983).

[3] A. J. P. Taylor, *The First World War* (London: Penguin Books), pp.180–1.

The truth about the introduction of convoy is that moves began as early as July 1916. Its introduction was a long drawn-out process fought out in the corridors of Whitehall but against the background of increasing merchant ship losses as the U-boat campaign began to take effect. While the Admiralty deliberated, the shocked survivors from sunken ships were coming ashore in British ports in ever-increasing numbers while the smoke of the U-boats' victims could be seen far out to sea.

Convoy was first introduced on the Harwich–Holland route, valuable not only for cargo but for the flow of intelligence from Europe. The merchant ships using this route were especially vulnerable given the proximity of significant German naval forces based at Ostend and Zeebrugge. In June 1916 the SS *Brussels* was captured and her Master, Captain Frayn, was subsequently executed by the Germans for attempting to resist capture. The next month another ship, the SS *Lestris*, was captured, and this provided that spur to introduce convoy for ships using this route.

On 16 July 1916 the decision was taken to use the cruisers and destroyers of the Harwich Force to escort merchant shipping on the Harwich–Holland route. The organization of these early convoys was initially fairly loose but it became gradually more controlled, with convoys sailing each way at six- to seven-day intervals. Between July 1916 and November 1918 there were 131 convoys on this route with 1,861 individual ship passages. Only six vessels were lost to enemy action, and none after June 1917 when the system was tightened up—a loss rate of 0.32 per cent.

The lessons of this early experiment were there for all to see but they went unheeded, for in September 1916 U-boats of the Flanders Flotilla sank over 50,000 tons of shipping in the English Channel without loss to themselves and despite the presence of 49 destroyers, 48 torpedo boats, seven Q-ships and 468 auxiliary vessels together with an unknown number of aircraft and airships. Yet the Admiralty were not unaware of the scale of the depredations on merchant shipping. Shortly before he became First Sea Lord in November 1916, Admiral Sir John Jellicoe submitted a memorandum on the subject entitled 'Submarine Menace' to the First Lord, his political superior, Arthur Balfour. Jellicoe argued that 'the serious and ever increasing menace is by far the most pressing question at the present time' and hinted that, if the worst came to the worst, the U-boats could force Britain to seek peace on disadvantageous terms. However, Jellicoe offered no new thinking on how to deal with the submarine threat other than more patrols, new weapons and the tactical routeing of shipping into 'safe' areas. When Lloyd George and others put the question of convoy to him, Jellicoe replied that it would not work because a convoy would present the U-boat with a bigger target and, in any case, merchant ships could not be relied upon to keep station.

It has been suggested by some historians that Lloyd George and his cabinet colleagues in favour of convoy, including Sir Edward Carson, who had replaced Balfour as First Lord of the Admiralty, did not stand up to the admirals by insisting on the introduction of convoy and that therefore he should share at least some of the responsibility for the ship losses. Such arguments show a lack of understanding of the constitutional relationship between the politicians and their service chiefs. Although it was within Lloyd George's powers as Prime Minister to insist that the Admiralty adopt convoy, it would have been unwise for him to do so. Lloyd George was already at loggerheads with the Army Council following the Battle of the Somme and had no wish to have the Admiralty Board ranged against him as well. In any case, such a course of action would have resulted in the resignation of the Admiralty Board—a Pyrrhic victory.

When Jellicoe became First Sea Lord in December 1916 he brought no new initiatives with him to combat the U-boat other than appointing Rear Admiral Alexander Duff to head the newly created Anti Submarine Division at the Admiralty. This apart, it was more of the same: more patrols, more aircraft and improved weaponry—all of which had a singular lack of success in both sinking U-boats and protecting the merchant ships. The introduction of the third campaign of unrestricted submarine warfare caused Lloyd George to try more persuasive tactics. He asked Sir Maurice Hankey, Secretary to the War Cabinet, to prepare a paper on the subject. Hankey's paper, produced with the objectivity of an outsider, was little short of a masterpiece. He quickly pointed out the fact that the Navy was already using the convoy system for important troopships and transports and that, indeed, the Grand Fleet never proceeded beyond the net barrages of Scapa Flow or Rosyth without its protective screen of destroyers. Hankey concluded:

> The adoption of the convoy system would appear to offer great opportunities for mutual support by the merchant vessels themselves, apart from the defence provided by their escorts. Instead of meeting one small gun on board one ship the enemy might be under fire from, say, ten guns distributed amongst twenty ships. Each merchant ship might have depth charges, and explosive charges in addition might be towed between pairs of ships, to be exploded electrically. One or two ships with paravanes might save a line of a dozen ships from the mine danger. Special salvage ships might accompany the convoy to salve those ships which were mined or torpedoed without sinking immediately and in any event to save the crews.[4]

Having read Hankey's paper, Lloyd George invited Jellicoe and Duff to a breakfast meeting which was also attended by Carson. The meeting was inconclusive but Jellicoe agreed to address a representative selection of ships' Masters about convoy on 23 February.

While the debate was going on about the merits of convoy in the corridors of Whitehall, another shipping route which had suffered greatly at the hands of the U-boats had quietly adopted the convoy system with markedly successful results. France required some 2 million tons of coal a month from

---

[4]*Ibid.*

Britain to make up for the loss of the coalfields in north-eastern France to German occupation, but by December 1916 the monthly shipments had declined to almost half of what was required. There was no lack of coal—on the contrary, supplies were plentiful—but it was all piled up in English ports because of the fear of submarine attack, the threat posed by the U-boats thus proving as effective as the activities of the craft themselves. An additional complication with the coal trade was the poorly organized routeing of ships: vessels loading at Newcastle were bound for Bordeaux while those destined to discharge cargo at Dunkerque were loaded at Bristol.

On 7 February 1917 'controlled sailings' were introduced for the French coal trade; evidently the word 'convoy' was too strong for Admiralty to stomach at this stage. Four routes were established:

1. Mount's Bay to Brest;
2. Weymouth to Cherbourg;
3. Weymouth to Le Havre; and
4. Dover/Folkestone to Calais/Boulogne.

The 'convoys' sailed at twenty-four hour intervals and were escorted by trawlers. The forces required for this duty were quite small—only fifteen trawlers were required for both Weymouth routes—and yet the results were dramatic. In March 1917 only three out of 1,500 ships engaged in the coal trade were lost, and by the end of April 1917 a force of 30 trawlers was covering over 4,000 channel crossings. By the end of the war 53 ships out of 39,352 had been lost—a rate of 0.13 per cent.

The introduction of convoy to the French coal trade was swiftly followed by its adoption for the Scandinavian trade route, which had suffered at the hands of both surface ships and U-boats. A conference at Longhope on 3 April 1917 recommended the introduction of convoy and the Admiralty grudgingly agreed. Twenty destroyers were allocated, together with seventy trawlers and drifters from the East Coast patrol. The Admiralty's reasons for consenting to the introduction of convoy on this route are puzzling when considered in the light of their resolute opposition to the general introduction of convoy. The argument that the nights were short in summer and therefore the ships would be better protected makes sense, but their view that convoy would be practicable since the ships would all have the same speed is incomprehensible. If this were true of the ships on the Scandinavian route, then why was it not true of the ships plying the other routes?

The organization of the Scandinavian convoy route was simple. Ships would assemble at Lerwick in the Shetland Islands and would be escorted across the North Sea to Norwegian waters where the convoy would disperse; the escort would wait at a pre-arranged rendezvous for the east-bound convoy and escort the ships back to Britain. The first convoy sailed on 29 April 1917. Convoys were initially quite small and consisted of six or seven ships, although this figure would later rise to twenty or twenty-five ships, escorted by two destroyers and four or five auxiliaries. As with the Dutch and French coal trade routes, the introduction of convoy on the Scandinavian route led to a drop in the numbers of ships lost. In May and June 1917, 1,871 ships were convoyed to and from Norwegian waters yet only six were lost—a rate of 0.3 per cent—and four of the losses were merchant ships *en route* to Lerwick from the Humber.

But greater events were afoot in April than the introduction of convoy on the Scandinavian route. On 6 April the United States, goaded beyond endurance by the activities of the U-boats, finally entered the war. Rear-Admiral William Sims, sent over to Europe to take command of US naval forces, was horrified when he discussed the shipping situation with Jellicoe on 9 April:

> I was fairly astounded; for I had never imagined anything so terrible. I expressed my consternation to Admiral Jellicoe. 'Yes,' he said, as quietly as though he was discussing the weather and not the future of the British Empire, 'it is impossible for us to go on with the war, if losses like this continue.'[5]

The German onslaught on merchant shipping reached its peak in April, with 881,027grt being sunk that month—27,704grt on 20 April alone. On 23 April Lloyd George raised the matter in Cabinet and was told that the only answer to the U-boat peril lay in more patrolling and the development of new weapons. The Admiralty refused to accept the fact that the patrols were inadequate: in the first four months of 1917 there had been thousands of attacks on submarines, real or suspected, but only eleven boats had been sunk and one of those (*UC32*) had blown up on her own mines. On 25 April the War Cabinet discussed the matter again and Lloyd George announced his intention to visit the Admiralty on 30 April.

In his *War Memoirs*, written after the war, Lloyd George was to claim that his decision to visit the Admiralty provided the vital impetus for the introduction of convoy. In this he is guilty of overstanding his case, for the decision to introduce it had been taken by the time he made his historic visit. Nevertheless, Lloyd George's visit undoubtedly concentrated the collective mind of the Admiralty.

Between 25 and 30 April events moved rapidly. In the afternoon of the 25th Admiral Duff, Director of the Anti Submarine Division, came to Jellicoe and presented a paper which pleaded for the introduction of convoy. Duff's case was so well researched and so cogently argued that the paper must have been weeks if not months in preparation. Duff proposed convoy for all vessels proceeding to Britain from the North and South Atlantic except those capable of speeds in excess of 15kts, which would be expected to rely on their speed for protection. Vessels would be convoyed from certain 'convoy depots' (Gibraltar, Dakar, Louisburg and Newport News) by merchant Q-ships. At a longitude well clear of the danger zone, the convoy would be met

---

[5]Sir Henry Newbolt, *Naval Operations*, vol. 5, (London: Longmans, 1928), p.357.

by an escort of destroyers and taken to a 'port of refuge' where it would disperse and the ships proceed to their destinations. Duff estimated that approximately 26 vessels a day would be passing through the danger zone and therefore some 45 vessels would be required for escort duties. He concluded:

> The larger the convoy passing through any given danger zone, provided it is moderately protected, the less the loss to the merchant services; that is, for instance, were it feasible to convoy the entire volume of trade which normally enter the UK *per diem* in one large group, the submarine as now working would be limited to one attack, which, with a destroyer escort, would result in negligible losses compared with those now being experienced.[6]

Truly Duff was on his personal road to Damascus. However, Jellicoe remained to be convinced: he would only go as far as authorizing a further study. On 27 April Jellicoe minuted the First Lord on the shipping situation. He did not mince his words:

> The real fact of the matter is this. We are carrying on the war at the present time as if we had the absolute command of the sea or anything approaching it. It is quite true that we are masters of the situation as far as surface ships are concerned but it must be realised, and realised at once, that such supremacy will be quite useless if the enemy's submarines paralyse us as they do now our lines of communication.[7]

Jellicoe's assessment of the situation was extraordinarily accurate yet his remedy was woefully inadequate. He proposed reductions in the numbers of lines of communications which the Navy was expected to guard, together with restrictions placed on the quantities of imports. But evidently the gravity of the situation finally convinced Jellicoe that convoy had to be tried, for on the same day he gave his blessing to Duff's paper. Thus by the time of Lloyd George visited the Admiralty he could be told that the latter had already decided to implement convoy. Honour was satisfied on both sides.

On 28 April the Senior Naval Officer at Gibraltar was notified that the UK-bound convoy would sail in ten days time. He was to select the appropriate merchant ships from those waiting to leave, with the following provisos:

1. The convoy was not exceed twenty vessels.

2. Each ship was to have a mean speed of 7kts and no ship should be capable of 11kts or above.

3. Each ship was fitted with a telephone linking bridge and engine room plates.

4. Each was to carry fog buoys and an RNVR signalman was to travel in each ship.

Sixteen ships were selected for this first convoy and their Masters attended the pre-sailing conference on 7 May which was addressed by the convoy

---

[6]Winton, p.65.

[7]Newbolt, p.357.

commodore, Captain H. C. Lockey RN, who would also command the escort, which consisted of the Q-ships *Mavis* and *Rule*.

In the evening of 10 May the convoy slipped out of Gibraltar. The ships were arranged in three columns 1,200yds apart, with Lockey leading the centre column in the *Clan Gordon*. Three armed yachts gace additional cover as far as 11°W. On 18 May the convoy was met off the Western Approaches by destroyers from Devonport and by a flying boat from the Scilly Isles. The port column of the convoy, which was composed of five merchant ships bound for ports on the West Coast of Britain, was detached on 20 May and proceeded independently, escorted by three destroyers. The remaining eleven ships proceeded to Portland, where the destroyers were replaced by twenty-four drifters. The convoy then proceeded in three divisions up-channel, arriving at The Downs on 22 May, where it was dispersed. Throughout the sailing of the convoy the station-keeping shown by the merchant ships had been excellent: distances between columns were never less than 1,000yds, thus allaying the Admiralty's suspicions on that point. The Masters commented that they had enjoyed more sleep during their passage than they had enjoyed for months.

Two days after the first Gibraltar–UK convoy arrived at The Downs, the first transatlantic convoy sailed from Hampton Roads. The first request for a transatlantic convoy had been made on 3 May when the Admiralty requested that the US Navy send a trial convoy of between sixteen and twenty merchant ships escorted by the six US destroyers currently under orders to proceed to Queenstown. Initially, the US Navy displayed all the reservations about convoy which had been aired on the other side of the Atlantic. The Americans preferred the defensive arming of merchant ships and felt that there was too much risk in allowing so many merchant ships to travel in one group. They were, however, to go as far as approving the sailing of small convoys of four ships with two escorts—a scheme which was accepted by the Admiralty until 22 May, when Their Lordships changed their collective mind, presumably as a result of the safe arrival of the Gibraltar convoy.

The first transatlantic convoy consisted of twelve ships escorted by the cruiser HMS *Roxburgh* (Captain F. A. Whitehead). Almost immediately this convoy provided a sharp reminder of the dangers threatening vessels which chose to sail independently. The merchant ships *Ravenshoe* and *Highbury* had to leave the convoy on account of being unable to keep up. On the return journey to Halifax the *Highbury* was torpedoed. Meanwhile the convoy itself proceeded, changing formation on 4 June from two columns in line astern of four ships and one of two ships to two front-facing columns of five ships, and when the convoy crossed the 20°W meridian on 5 June the ships began to zigzag in formation. The next day the escort was augmented by eight destroyers from Devonport and the whole formation proceeded up-channel. On 8 June ships bound for West Coast ports were detached off the Smalls and next day the remainder came to anchor off St Helen's in the Isle of Wight. In his report of proceedings, Captain Whitehead paid tribute to the seamanship displayed by the merchantmen and concluded by saying that he would happily take a convoy of thirty ships across the Atlantic.

Four more convoys left Hampton Roads in quick succession, on 4, 12, 19 and 25 June, with twelve, eleven, eighteen and twenty ships respectively. The ships were mainly tankers (Britain was experiencing a severe fuel shortage), and of the 61 ships convoyed only one, the *Washaba*, was torpedoed but she managed to return to harbour. It seems that the U-boat, distracted by the activities of the escort, fired only a 'browning' shot. Surely nothing demonstrated the success of convoy so much as the fact that 60 out of 61 valuable tankers and their valuable cargoes had reached harbour: before the introduction of convoy, fifteen of them would probably have been sunk.

As the convoy system developed at sea, so the administrative machine ashore required to organize the mass of shipping evolved. On 15 May it was decided to set up the Atlantic Trade Convoy Committee to supervise convoy arrangements. The members were Captain H. W. Longden, Fleet Paymaster H. W. E. Manisty, Commander J. S. Wilde, Lieutenant G. E. Burton and Mr Norman Leslie of the Ministry of Shipping. On 6 June the Committee reported with proposals.

The responsibility for running the convoy system was to be that of the Assistant Chief of the Naval Staff, although in September 1917 this would be transferred to the Director of Mercantile Movements. Fleet Paymaster Manisty became the organizing manager of convoys, responsible for the control of sailings, the preparation of programmes, the appointment of convoy commodores and drawing up the orders for the escorts. Commander J. W. Carrington was appointed Officer in Charge of the Chart Room, with day-to-day responsibility for the routeing of convoys and the avoidance of known danger areas. Port Convoy Officers were appointed in each convoy assembly and dispersal port.

At this stage the Committee's proposals concerned the Atlantic sea route only. Homeward-bound convoys would assemble at New York, Hampton Roads, Dakar and Gibraltar. The Committee hoped that two convoys would run every eight days, sailing alternately for East and West Coast ports. The composition of the convoys was restricted to ships with a speed of more than 8kts but less than 12: any other ships had to take their chance sailing independently. Fourteen flotillas of escorts would be required for the close escort and 52 cruisers or armed merchant cruisers for the ocean escort. These proposals were formally approved on 14 June 1917. By the end of July 1917, 244 ships had reached the United Kingdom from North American ports in thirteen convoys with the loss of only two ships, one of which, the *Whitehall*, was sunk after she had strayed from the convoy. One of these convoys, HH.23 from Hampton Roads, carried cargoes such as steel, sugar, oil, nitrates, sulphur and wheat— materials at the heart of the war effort. Beginning on 11 August, the convoy system was extended to South Atlantic

TABLE 5: CO-ORDINATION OF CONVOYS, AUGUST 1917[8]

Outward convoy	Date of sailing	Homeward convoy met by escort	Date of RV with homeward escort	Original sailing date of home-ward convoy
OM.1	13 Aug	HG.5	17 Aug	10 Aug
OD.1	16 Aug	HH.4	18 Aug	3 Aug
OB.1	17 Aug	HS.5	20 Aug	10 Aug
OF.1	18 Aug	HG.6	21 Aug	15 Aug
OM.2	18 Aug	–	–	–
OD.2	20 Aug	HL.1	23 Aug	12 Aug

traffic, largely as a result of a cruise by *U155* (Lt-Cdr Mensel) during which she sank nineteen ships in waters off the Azores and the 43rd parallel, which showed that the Germans were extending their operations further afield.

Although the system for homeward-bound convoys seemed to be operating successfully, the problem of protecting outward-bound shipping had yet to be dealt with. There was little use in convoying a merchant ship and its precious cargo to Britain only to have the same ship lost on her next outward passage while sailing independently. The U-boat commanders noted this weak point and seized on it. In April 1917 the ratio of sinkings to sailings in homeward traffic was 18 per cent and in outward traffic 7 per cent, but by September that year the homeward sinkings were falling and the outward ones rising. The problem had been appreciated in some quarters at the Admiralty as early as July 1917 but resistance to the idea of escorting the outward traffic was immense: one officer went so far as to minute that the reason so many outward-bound ships were being sunk was that the patrols had been discontinued to provide escorts for convoys.

The solution was to give the outward-bound ships the same degree of protection afforded to the homeward-bound traffic. However, this would in theory double the number of escorts required. The answer was simple. The escort for the outward-bound convoy would accompany it to its dispersal point outside the danger zone aiming, to leave the convoy at sunset. The destroyers would then steam through the night to a pre-arranged rendezvous with the homeward-bound convoy at daybreak. The system was beautifully simple, but it was very demanding on the escorts and required that the convoy timetables be substantially revised.

The assembly ports for outward convoys were Devonport, Queenstown, Lamlash/Buncrana, Falmouth and Milford Haven. The system became immensely complicated since outward sailings now had to be co-ordinated with the arrival of homeward-bound convoys while leaving the escort sufficient time to steam from dispersal point to rendezvous. The first outward-bound convoy sailed from Milford Haven on 13 August and Table 5 shows how tightly co-ordinated the system quickly became.

---

[8] Winton, p.87.

TABLE 6: CONVOY SYSTEMS, SUMMER 1917

From	Code	Frequency	Speed (kts)
Homeward-bound			
Hampton Roads	HH	Every 8 days to W. and E. Coast ports alternately	8
Sydney (Cape Breton)	HS	Every 8 days to W. and E. Coast ports alternately	8
New York	HN	Every 8 days to E. coast	9½
New York	HX	Every 8 days to W. coast	13
Quebec	HC	Every 8 days to W. and E. Coast ports alternately	11½
New York	HB	Every 8 days to Biscay ports	8
Sierra Leone	HL	Every 8 days to either coast	10
Dakar	HD	Every 8 days to either coast	8
Gibraltar	HG	Every 4 days to W. and E. Coast ports alternately	7
Outward-bound			
Lamlash	OB	Every 8 days	8
Liverpool	OLB	Every 8 days northward	8
Liverpool	OLX	Every 8 days northward	13
Liverpool	OL	Every 8 days southward	10
Milford	OM	Every 4 days	7½
Falmouth	OF	Every 8 days	7½
Devonport	OD	Every 3 days	8
Southend	OC	Every 16 days	11½

Thus, despite its hesitant start in May 1917, convoy grew with an impetus that was all its own (see Table 6). By the end of the First World War approximately 90 per cent of all coastal and ocean shipping was in convoy. The French, Dutch and Scandinavian trade routes were in convoy. There were many convoy systems operating in the Mediterranean—Gibraltar–Genoa, Alexandria–Bizerta, Port Said–Syracuse, Port Said–UK (sailing alternately to East and West Coast ports) and Liverpool–Port Said. The Atlantic route had the most complex pattern of all. Once started, the convoy system could not be halted, for the lessons were clear for all to see.

In June 1917 merchant shipping losses had reached their second highest peak—286 ships totalling 696,720 tons. Thereafter the statistics show a steady decline (see Table 7). The rate of loss diminished significantly after August, the September figure being nearly one-third less than that for August and not much more than half the monthly average for the period

TABLE 7: MERCHANT SHIP LOSSES, JULY–DECEMBER 1917

Month	Tonnage lost	U-boats sunk
July	555,514	6
August	472,372	5
September	353,602	11
October	466,542	5
November	302,599	8
December	411,766	8
Total	2,562,395	43

TABLE 8: MERCHANT SHIP LOSSES, JANUARY–NOVEMBER 1918			
Month	Tonnage	No of ships sunk	U-boats sunk
Jan	295,630	160	10
Feb	335,202	138	2
March	368,746	190	6
April	300,069	134	6
May	296,558	139	14
June	268,505	110	3
July	280,820	113	6
Aug	310,180	154	7
Sept	171,972	91	9
Oct	116,237	73	5
Nov	10,233	3	1
Total	2,754,152	1,305	69

February–May. The total of ships lost in the last quarter of the year (235, grossing 702,799 tons) was little more than half that of the peak quarter (413 ships, totalling 1,315,496 tons). Clearly, the critical stage in the *Handelskrieg* was over, even if losses were exceeding replacements.

In this respect the situation was still very serious. In May 1917 Sir Leo Chiozza Money, the Government's shipping adviser, had calculated that 4,812,000 tons of shipping was the irreducible minimum necessary for the importation of basic foodstuffs. The total available at the beginning of April was 8,394,000 tons, but over the following nine months 2,909,155 tons had been sunk while only 917,000 tons of new shipping had been added to the register. The balance of British shipping available for the import of foodstuffs at the end of 1917 was, therefore, 6,401,845 tons. However, included in this figure was 925,000 tons of shipping which had been damaged, and most of these vessels would be out of service for periods of between four and six months. This left only 5,476,845 tons available—only 664,845 tons above the irreducible minimum. The situation remained precarious.

Nevertheless, sinkings were declining and it was the convoy system which was responsible: it was certainly not because of any significant increase in the number of U-boats sunk. Between July and December 1917, 44 U-boats were sunk while a further 55 were commissioned. Clearly, the U-boat force was thriving—if only in terms of numbers of boats available for operations.

In 1918 the downward pattern of shipping losses continued (see Table 8). U-boat losses remained fairly constant—proof that the convoy system was succeeding in bringing the vital supplies and troops from America which the country needed. This was the essence of the problem as Professor Arthur Marder as so succinctly put it:

> Sinking submarines is a bonus not a necessity . . . what matters is that ships deliver cargoes regularly and adequately . . . Indeed one can safely go a step further: it really did not matter how many U-boats the Germans had, if they were forced to keep out of the way and the British and their Allies got their

ships and their literally vital cargoes through and without being delayed by fear of attack.[9]

Since the introduction of ocean convoy, the U-boats had moved their operations to inshore waters where they could prey on unescorted ships sailing independently or about to join or having departed from an ocean convoy. This shows how the convoy system was able to act offensively by imposing an operating method on the aggressor. In June 1918 this loophole was finally blocked with the introduction of the convoy system to the East Coast and Irish Sea trade. Another factor affecting the U-boats, and one that was growing in importance, was the provision of air cover to convoys in coastal waters. Between June and October 1918, 564 aircraft, seaplanes and airships flew 87,803 hours in support of convoys, sighted 167 U-boats and made 155 attacks. Though air power made little contribution to the number of U-boats sunk—airborne weapons were too small and too inaccurate to do a U-boat serious harm—it represented a considerable deterrent. The sight of a distant tethered kite balloon or patrolling aircraft or seaplane usually caused a U-boat commander to think twice.

Aircraft played an important part in forcing the U-boats to make one last change to their *modus operandi*. From June 1918 they began to move their activities out into the distant Western Approaches, beyond the range of aircraft. When they came in contact with a convoy they found their efforts frustrated by their low dived speed and the vigilance of the escorts. Consequently they now began making their attacks from the surface at night—a tactic which would only be developed fully in the next war.

By the end of 1917 the convoy system had won a war-winning victory—even if the results were not fully apparent to those who did not wish to see. The figures show how the introduction of the convoy system saved Britain from capitulation. But they represent an abstract picture of a campaign that was fought at sea. Just how did the convoy system work in practice, and what did its introduction mean for the men of the U-boats?

---

[9]Newbolt, *Naval Operations*, vol.4, p.104.

CHAPTER FIVE

Defeating the U-Boats

It was clear to me what a monstrous superiority of material and force had been used to defeat us. — Karl Dönitz, Commanding Officer, *UB68*

T O MOST naval officers who had initially been sceptical of convoy, the wonder of it all was that it worked. None of the administrative fears about merchant ships being needlessly detained while waiting for convoy was realized. Ships waiting for convoy had their names placed at the back of a card index system held at each convoy port. When their cards came to front of the 'pack' they would join the next available and appropriate convoy. The system was simple and it worked. Fears about the incompetence of the Merchant Navy proved groundless. Sub-Lieutenant Roger Goldrich RN, First Lieutenant of the sloop HMS *Poppy*, was a typical officer in his attitudes to the merchant service, as his 1917 diary entries show:

> 4th August: Escorted our convoy to 16°W with complete success and left them at 11.30pm to rendezvous with the Isis having a convoy of 22 large merchant vessels.

> 15th August: Picked up the convoy at 8.15 . . . took station on the starboard quarter of convoy which is zig-zagging at nine knots. I have never seen so many merchant ships together and the marvel of it is that they are keeping station about four cables apart and zig-zagging with almost the precision of the fleet.[1]

If mistakes did occur, they were as often the fault of the escort as of the merchant ships. Goldrich recalls that, on 19 October 1917, when heading for the rendezvous point for an inbound convoy, he

> Spent a miserable middle watch with a bilious attack. Neuralgia and vomiting ad lib. Passed convoy about 1pm in fog and ran about another 30 miles W. Now we are crashing E at 15 knots to overtake them. A first class balls is what the SO [Senior Officer] in the Ossory had made of this lot.[2]

Inevitably there were mix-ups, both the escorts and the merchant ships being new to the sort of manoeuvres required. Occasionally the confusion had a humorous side. An eastbound and a westbound convoy passed close to one another in thick fog in the Mediterranean, near the Strait of Gibraltar, and there was considerable confusion. When all had settled down and both

---

[1]Papers of Sub-Lieutenant Roger Goldrich RN, Department of Documents, Imperial War Museum.

[2]*Ibid.*

convoys were on their way, one ship in the eastbound group realized that something was amiss and was told, 'My convoy's going to Salonika—where are you going?'

The escorts were generally effective in keeping the U-boats away. Should a U-boat manage to make an attack (see below for an analysis of how difficult this could be), then it invariably gave away its position. On Christmas Day 1917 *U87* (von Speth-Schulzberg) fired at a ship in convoy. The sloop *Buttercup* ran down the torpedo track and rammed her. *U87* escaped, though was damaged, but was sighted again by the patrol vessel *PC56*, which rammed her for a second time, cutting her in two. The bow and stern sections were vigorously shelled by both *Buttercup* and *PC56* before they sank. There were no survivors.

The improvement in morale among the men of the Merchant Navy was immense, particularly when they saw the escort engaging in a depth-charge attack against the enemy which had dogged them for months. The value of the escort in dealing with U-boats was evident in ways other than attacking them. On 14 November 1917 the armed merchant cruiser *Marmora* was escorting a homeward-bound convoy from Dakar when she sighted a U-boat on the surface ahead of the convoy. By ordering avoiding action *Marmora* was able to shepherd her charges away from the danger.

However, a determined commander would get through. Perhaps the most striking example of a determined U-boat attack on a convoy is the sinking of the liner *Justicia* on 19 July 1918. *Justicia* was one of seven ships, escorted by nine destroyers, in the fast outward-bound convoy OLX.39, the so-called 'Liverpool Express'. The ships were disposed in three columns of two, the starboard column being composed of three ships. *Justicia* was the lead ship in the starboard inner column, and shortly after 3.30 p.m. she was torpedoed by *UB64* (von Schrader) which had penetrated the screen.

Justicia had been hit in the engine room on the port side, and, losing speed, dropped out of the column. Six of the close-escort destroyers circled round her, dropping depth charges. At 5.30 p.m. a tug arrived and began to take the crippled liner in tow. Von Schrader, however, had not been put off by the destroyers' counter-attack: he made two more attacks without scoring any hits before having to break off because of damage.

Von Schrader did not remain inactive. Throughout the night of 19–20 July the tugs and destroyers nursed the stricken liner back towards Liverpool. *UB64* broadcast reports in the hope that another boat could finish her off. On 20 July the group of ships was intercepted by *U54* (von Rucketschall), who put two torpedoes into her. Three hours later *Justicia* rolled over and sank. *U54* got away, despite broaching after the attack, but the escorts found some compensation in sinking *UB124* (Wutsdorf), which was in the area having also heard von Schrader's action report.

The most vulnerable time for a convoy was while it was forming up or dispersing, when the merchant ships were disorganized and the screen not properly effective. The German *Torpedo Firing Manual* for 1918 commented on the 'indescribable irregularity in station-keeping at the point of assembly . . . threatening mutual ramming'.[3] The defences at Lamlash (Lough Swilly) were incomplete when outward-bound convoys began at the end of August 1917, so the ships sailed from Buncrana. On 21 August a convoy of 21 steamers left the harbour in single file to form up, escorted by two cruisers and six destroyers. At noon the *Devonian* was torpedoed, followed shortly afterwards by the *Roscommon*, while the *Vasari* was missed. The convoy put back into harbour and the commodore later emphasized the dangers always present when a convoy of ships nearly twelve miles long was forming up in unprotected waters. The U-boat escaped. Fortunately this was an isolated incident, and it is puzzling why, given that they were well aware of this weakness in the system, the Germans did not make greater efforts to exploit it.

Convoy was not, however, an infallible solution. Two possibilities had to be borne in mind, first that a U-boat would penetrate the screen and sink most of the ships inside (although in fact this never happened), and second that the escort would be overwhelmed by a superior enemy surface force which would then proceed to attack the convoy. The Scandinavian convoys were always more vulnerable to attack. Although the route was short it was totally within the submarine danger zone and within striking distance of German bases. Moreover the German consuls in Norwegian ports were able to report on sailing dates and the composition of convoys and escorts. Despite these built-in disadvantages, however, the Scandinavian convoys ran successfully until October 1917 when the Admiralty, aware through signals intelligence that the Germans were plotting a raid, ordered Admiral Sir David Beatty, Commander-in-Chief of the Grand Fleet, to set patrols well to the south of the convoy route to intercept any German ships coming north.

On 15 October 1915 an east-bound convoy left Lerwick escorted by the destroyers *Mary Rose* and *Strongbow* with two trawlers. Shortly before noon on 16 October *Mary Rose* went on ahead of the convoy to collect the west-bound convoy while *Strongbow* stayed with the ships until they dispersed and then returned to meet *Mary Rose* with the return convoy, which consisted of twelve ships (two British, one Belgian, one Spanish, five Danish and three Swedish). By dawn on 17 October the convoy was proceeding nicely, with *Mary Rose* about seven or eight miles ahead and with *Strongbow* on the convoy's port beam. Neither destroyer was aware that a state of alert existed in the North Sea.

Just after 6 a.m. *Strongbow*'s lookouts sighted two ships coming up from the south which shortly afterwards opened fire. The two vessels were the German minelaying cruisers *Brummer* and *Bremse*, which had steamed north, undetected by all the patrols, to attack the convoy. It was known by Room

---

[3]*Torpedo Firing from Submarines* (Submarine School, Kiel, February 1917), p.75.

40, the Admiralty's signals intelligence centre, that the two ships were at sea, but nothing was done to warn Beatty since it was assumed that they were on a minelaying operation—because they were thus fitted.

Strongbow was repeatedly hit and had to be abandoned. *Mary Rose*, hearing the gunfire behind her, turned back was engaged by the German ships. Despite putting up a gallant resistance she was overwhelmed and sank. As she was going down her commanding officer, Lt-Cdr Charles Fox RN, shouted 'God bless my heart lads, get her going again—we're done yet!' *Brummer* and *Bremse* then rolled up the convoy, sinking nine ships (all the Scandinavian vessels, totalling 10,248 tons) before heading for home.

Though the gallant defence offered by *Mary Rose* and *Strongbow* was heralded in the British press as heroic and compared with the deeds of Sir Richard Grenville in the *Revenge*, nothing could conceal the fact that the incident represented a complete disaster. The two German ships had steamed the length of the North Sea and back through waters patrolled by eighty British warships and had sunk two destroyers and nine merchant ships before returning home. The German press was jubilant while the Scandinavian countries were torn between blaming German brutality and British carelessness.

Yet despite the lessons of this *Mary Rose* incident and the general tightening up the system which followed it, there was another calamity on the Scandinavian route on 15 December 1917 when German destroyers of the Third Half Flotilla engaged a convoy of one British and five neutral merchant ships escorted by the destroyers *Pellew* and *Partridge*, sinking all of them before heading home, neatly avoiding the ships of the 3rd Light Cruiser Squadron on the way.

The incident aroused a considerable furore in the press and in Parliament and the Admiralty was forced to order a court of enquiry. In this context it is interesting to note how the loss of six merchant ships in convoy became a cause for Government action while the veritable massacre of British merchant shipping eight months earlier had gone almost unnoticed. The results of the enquiry were that the Admiralty assumed direct management for the running of the Scandinavian convoys, which now sailed every three days instead of daily so that only one convoy would be at sea at a time, thus relieving the Grand Fleet of the problem of having to provide two sets of escorts. The sailing port would be moved down to Methil, which shortened the route by eighty miles though brought it nearer the German bases.

The problems attendant on the Scandinavian convoys were unusual. Generally speaking, convoys continued to run without such spectacular interference. In doing so they achieved a war-winning victory. Yet it was a victory that went almost unheralded. Unlike the campaign on the Western Front, there no great offensives, only the ceaseless grind of sailings, patrols, zigzagging and screening, often carried out in foul weather and with only an isolated U-boat sighting.

By the end of September 1917 it was clear that Holtzendorff's pledge to strangle Britain's economic lifelines had failed. Yet his U-boats had done what was asked of them and had sunk a theoretical amount of tonnage. What had gone wrong? First, Holtzendorff had greatly underestimated the skill with which the British organized their merchant marine, in defiance of all economic and commercial logic. Better use was being made of the existing shipping without any reductions in the numbers of ships committed for military use. Shipping was concentrated in short routes, like that across the North Atlantic, and imports were restricted to what was necessary. Though this caused some inconvenience on the British home front it was nothing compared to the privations brought about by the British blockade in Germany. The second reason for the failure of the German offensive was convoy. Although the Germans carried on sinking a significant number of ships, they were sinking them in the wrong places, away from the main sea lanes, as the convoy system spread. That they had failed to achieve their ends was evident to the Germans, but however much the Deputies in the *Reichstag* complained about the failure of the offensive they could not shake the German High Command. It was, like the land offensive of March 1918, one of the Germans' last cards, and once it had been dealt there were no alternatives. They had staked their all on the success of unrestricted submarine warfare, and they would just have to continue with it.

For the U-boats, the introduction of the convoy system had instant effects. The seas which had been crowded with shipping were now empty. As one U-boat commander wrote,

> The oceans at once became bare and empty: for long periods at a time U-boats, operating individually, would see nothing at all; and then suddenly up would loom a huge convoy of ships, thirty or fifty or more of them, surrounded by a strong escort of warships of all types. The solitary U-boat, which most probably had sighted the convoy purely by chance, would attack, thrusting again and again and persisting, if the commander had strong nerves, for perhaps several days and nights, until the physical exhaustion of both crew and commander called a halt. The lone U-boat might well sink one or two of the ships or even several; but that was a poor percentage of the whole. The convoy would steam on. In most cases no other U-boat would catch sight of it, and it would reach Britain, bringing a rich cargo of foodstuffs and raw materials safely to port.[4]

However, this particular officer had learned the lessons of the First World War extremely well: Karl Dönitz would go on to command Germany's U-boats in the next war with devastating effect, although the convoy system, coupled with technology, would defeat his boats in the same way as they were defeated in 1914–1918. Dönitz, though, was being optimistic here: in 69 of the 84 ocean convoys attacked only one ship was sunk, in twelve convoys two ships were sunk and in each of the remaining three convoys three ships were sunk. The U-boat could seldom linger in the area for a second shot.

---

[4]K. Dönitz, *Memoirs: Ten Years and Twenty Days* (London, 1959), p.4.

Dönitz's own submarine, *UB68*, was sunk while attacking a convoy. On 4 October 1918 he had encountered a west-bound convoy 150 miles east of Malta and had sunk the 3,883-ton *Oopack* in a surface attack shortly before dawn. As the sun came up Dönitz dived the boat to make a second submerged attack. However, the boat broached in full view of the convoy escorts and Dönitz ordered all tanks to be flooded in a very quick dive. The boat plunged down to 102 metres before the engineer officer could check her descent and she then shot to the surface like a cork. She was unable to dive because all her compressed air had been exhausted, so, amid a hail of gunfire from the escorts, Dönitz ordered the seacocks opened and his crew to abandon ship. *UB68* sank in seconds and Dönitz and his crew were picked up by HMS *Snapdragon*.

Dönitz's views on the convoy system were echoed by another U-boat commander, Lt-Cdr Saalwachter of *U91*:

> The convoys, with their strong and efficient escorts making an attack extremely difficult, are in my view quite capable of drastically reducing shipping losses. The chances of sighting a convoy of seven ships are less than sighting seven independent ships. In the case of a convoy it is mostly possible to fire on only one ship. For any ship torpedoed in convoy, the chance of immediate help is a factor of considerable importance to morale.[5]

The presence of the escorts with their arsenal of depth charges undoubtedly exercised a deterrent effect. The American Rear-Admiral William Sims, Commander-in-Chief of US naval forces in Europe, believed that for every submarine sighted by a destroyer there were many which sighted destroyers and then avoided them.

In attacking a convoy the U-boat was beset with problems. Because of its low underwater endurance it was unable to make a submerged approach unless the convoy were sighted well before the beam: anything else left the U-boat exposed to a stern chase which would drain her battery. The only alternative for the commander was to surface and make an 'end-around' the convoy to a favourable position, then submerge and wait. This is what the U-boat sighted by *Marmora* (see above) was probably doing. The disadvantages were that the boat could be sighted and attacked and that avoiding action could be taken by the convoy.

Even if the commander managed to gain an attacking position, his problems were not yet over. The positions from which he could attack were dictated by his submarine's speed and the performance of his torpedoes. If the escorts were disposed around the convoy with these parameters in mind, then he would have to penetrate the screen, remain in the attack area long enough to identify a target, aim and fire while at the same time taking care not to betray his position to the escorts by the incautious use of periscope or by inadvertently breaking surface. Once he managed to fire, then the

---

[5]Admiral A. Spindler, *Die Handelskrieg mit U-booten*, vol. 4 (Berlin, 1935), p.224.

explosion of the torpedo (or merely its track) would act as a 'flaming datum' for the alert escorts. The U-boat would have to withdraw in the presence of the alerted escorts, who would be operating within the ranges of detection and performance of their own equipment. It was no easy task being a U-boat commander. Depth-charge attacks undoubtedly exerted considerable psychological pressure on the U-boats. 'Never as long as I live will I forget those convoy attacks . . . I do not know if I possess the power to convey the maddening nervous strain which an attack like this imposed,'[6] wrote Commander Ernst Hashagen, Commanding Officer of *U62*, who was an extremely experienced commander.

The ordeal of *UB72* in May 1918 can be taken as being a fairly typical illustration of how the tables had been turned on the U-boats. On 7 and 8 May a total of 51 depth charges were dropped on *UB72*. The first three were from an airship and did no damage. The submarine was then pursued by a destroyer which dropped a further 23 charges, rupturing a fuel tank and causing the submarine to leave a trail of oil. Next day the boat was attacked by another destroyer with twenty depth charges, and then, just when *UB72* thought herself safe, she was depth-charged by a motor launch.

U98 had a similar tale to tell. In the course of a 23-day patrol in the Irish Sea in June 1918 she sank one small neutral ship but was continually harassed by the Royal Navy. Three days out from Emden she was attacked by a British submarine but the torpedo missed. Two days later she was attacked again by a submarine. On the tenth day of her patrol she was twice depth-charged by destroyers escorting first a lone large merchant ship and then a convoy. *U98* was next assaulted from the air when an airship escorting a convoy straddled her with bombs while she was attempting to make an 'end-around' on a convoy. In Cardigan Bay she was depth charged by a flotilla of hydrophone-equipped motor launches and she was then attacked by another British submarine. Her final attempt to inflict some damage was swiftly ended when the noise of her motors was picked up by an escort which delivered a depth-charge attack.

It was small wonder that U-boat commanders looked gaunt and haggard after a patrol. In addition to the counter-attacks by British anti-submarine forces, the threat posed by the barrage defences in the Strait of Dover, the Strait of Otranto and the North Sea was always at the back of their minds. Although the determined commander could, and did, find a way through, the risk of being mined or caught in a net was ever present. It says much for their courage that they continued.

The truth was that convoys had wrested the initiative from the U-boats, which could no longer simply patrol the trade routes and roll up the targets as they had done in the heady days of 1917. Instead they had to find the heavily escorted convoys. Their tactics were wholly reactive. On the introduction of

---

[6]Commander E. Hashagen, *The Log of a U-boat Commander* (London, 1931), pp.227–8.

convoys they moved to coastal waters and concentrated on unescorted outward-bound traffic. When outward-bound and coastal convoys were introduced they moved further afield, off the American coast and down towards the Azores. And the increasing effectiveness of convoy defences forced them to conduct their attacks at night—with all the problems that that entailed.

The only attempt by the U-boats to regain the initiative came with plans for them to work in groups. In May 1917, when the initial experience with British convoys showed that a single U-boat had only a slender chance against a strong defence, *Fregattenkapitän* Hermann Bauer, *FdU* of the High Seas Fleet submarines, suggested that several boats should operate jointly. For this purpose he wanted to put a flotilla commander on one of the large U-boats of the *U151* class, which was to be fitted with additional wireless equipment, and allow him to act as tactical commander in order to co-ordinate attacks on convoys by several boats at once.

Bauer was relieved of his command before his plan could be put into effect, but his successor, *Kapitän zur See* Andreas Michelsen, implemented the plan, though without the element of tactical control provided by the command U-boat. Between 10 and 25 May 1918 a group of about a dozen boats congregated off the Western Approaches. The operation was not a success, despite a procession of convoys through the area. Five vessels were sunk, but during the same period 183 ships were convoyed safely to the UK while 110 were safely escorted outwards. The best opportunity was offered to *U70*, which attempted to attack convoy HS.38 from Halifax escorted by eight destroyers and three sloops. The commander was presented with an almost perfect opportunity. Weather conditions were good, with a clear sky and enough wind to ruffle the waves and hide the distinctive periscope 'feather', and the convoy covered a wide front, yet all the commander could do was fire two torpedoes at the rear ship in the starboard wing column and then break off the action. In return the Germans lost *U103*, rammed and sunk by the *Olympic*, and *UB72*, torpedoed and sunk by the British submarine *D4*, both on 11 May 1918.

Combined attacks were also tried in the Mediterranean by Otto Steinbauer, another 'ace', in *U48*, but these were no more successful. A lack of efficient communication was the main reason—a deficiency which would be put right in the next war.

The U-boat commanders had no real answer to convoy but to carry on as conditions became steadily tougher for them. U-boat losses were never really a problem—they were always exceeded by new construction—but the loss of trained personnel (and the subsequent dilution of crews) was. Commanding officers like Arnauld de la Perière and Hashagen were having to go to sea with young and inexperienced crews. Other problems for the U-boat commanders included the difficulties posed by night attacks, the denial of surface running during the day because of the incessant ASW activity and the frustration of seeing an empty sea day after day. Despite the strain, however, there is no evidence that there was ever a crisis of morale in the U-boat forces—rather a dogged determination to see the job done.

35▲   36▲

35. Vice-Admiral A. H. Duff, head of the Anti Submarine Division and a last-minute convert to the virtues of convoy.

36. Admiral Sir John Jellicoe, First Sea Lord, who only consented to the introduction of convoy as a last desperate measure.

37. An aerial photograph of a convoy zigzagging in British coastal waters.

37▼

▲38 ▼39

38. A damaged merchant ship, down by the stern after being torpedoed, is escorted by two trawlers. Note the two gun positions at the stern; the starboard gun itself appears to be missing.

39. A merchant ship breaks up after being torpedoed.

40. An airship over a convoy. Airships were a very useful component of the escort and a considerable deterrent to U-boats.

41. 'The Yanks are here!'—the crew of the destroyer USS *Drayton* at Queenstown in 1918. On the American entry into the war, US escorts were deployed in European waters and proved very useful.

41 ▼

▲ 42   ▼ 43

42. An Atlantic convoy with an air escort during the final stage of its journey, 1918.
43. Convoy operations continued in all weathers: an American destroyer rolling in heavy seas, 1918.
44. An American destroyer escorts a convoy across the Atlantic in 1918.
45. The liner *Justicia*, torpedoed on 18 July 1918 after a series of determined U-boat attacks.
46. A Scandinavian convoy at sea. Such convoys faced special problems.

44 ▲

45▲   46▼

▲47　▼48

47. The destroyer HMS *Strongbow* which, along with HMS *Mary Rose*, was sunk by the German cruiser-minelayers *Brummer* and *Bremse* in the disaster of 17 October 1917.

48. *Admiral* von Holtzendorff. His predictions about the success of the campaign were not fulfilled.

49. A 'Standard' type merchant ship coming off the ways at Sunderland in 1918. Standardization of merchant ship construction was one way in which the shipping shortage was overcome.

50. The success of convoy: a merchant ship unloads her cargo at Liverpool after an Atlantic crossing.

▲51   ▼52

51. A British Army supply dump in France. All these supplies came by sea at some stage and without convoy the ability of the Army to carry on the war would have been in doubt.
52. American troops arrive at Le Havre in 1918. Convoy ensured the safe transport of the American Army to Europe.
53. Victory: the White Ensign flies over a surrendered German U-boat at Harwich in November 1918.
54. A forlorn trot of U-boats interned at Harwich at the end of the war.

53▲   54▼

▲55 ▼56

55. The steel mill at Yawata on Kyushu, which produced nearly 7 million tons of steel a year. The mill depended on imports of ore and coal to keep it going.

56. Japanese infantry occupy the oilfields in the Dutch East Indies early in 1942. The desire to secure the mineral wealth of the region was the prime motive behind Japanese expansion.

57. The attack on Pearl Harbor, 7 December 1941, which brought the Americans into the war.

58. The ship's company of USS *Trout* unload gold evacuated from the Philippines. Such operations were important in the early days of the war but detracted from commerce raiding.

59. A battered 'S' boat returns to Brisbane after a patrol off the Solomons in 1942. Note the 'pitting' on the conning tower, indicative of the boat's age.
60. Admiral Charles A. Lockwood (left), commander of the US submarines of the Pacific Fleet and the driving force behind the wartime campaign.
61. The Japanese destroyer *Yamakaze* sinking on 25 June 1942 after being torpedoed by USS *Nautilus*.
62. An 'S' boat arrives at Dutch Harbor, Alaska, after a patrol off the Aleutians. The crews of these boats endured extremes of heat and cold.

▲59   ▼60

▲ 63

63. Admiral Chester W. Nimitz, Commander-in-Chief of the US Pacific Fleet, awards the Navy Cross to Lt-Cdr Thomas Klakring USN of USS *Guardfish* for his successful patrol in Japanese waters.

64. USS *Bass* on completion. She was the first of the fleet boats.

65. USS *Porpoise*, a 'P' class submarine, on completion. The 'P' class set the mark for subsequent construction.

▼ 64

▼ 65

66 ▲

67 ▲

68 ▲

66. USS *Salmon* in August 1944, showing wartime additions including a cut-down conning tower, radar masts, Oerlikon guns on sponsons and a 5in gun aft of the conning tower.
67. USS *Trout*, a 'T' class submarine built by Electric Boat at Groton, under way as completed. The 'Ts' were the last class to be completed before the war.
68. USS *Greenling*, one of the very successful *Gato/Balao* group, as completed with the characteristic large and bulky conning tower.
69. USS *Hawkbill* carrying a very heavy surface armament of two 5in guns, fore and aft of the conning tower, one 40mm Bofors on the forward sponson and a 20mm Oerlikon on the after sponson.

69 ▼

70. USS *Billfish*, a *Balao* class boat, goes down the ways at Portsmouth Navy Yard in 1943. By now five US submarines were being commissioned a month.

71. Three *Balao* class submarines ready to be floated out of No 1 Dock at Portsmouth, New Hampshire, 27 January 1944—from left to right, *Redfish*, *Ronquil* (being 'christened') and *Razorback*. Portsmouth did not repeat the experiment of building three boats in the one dock; it was found to be quicker to build two per dock.

▼71

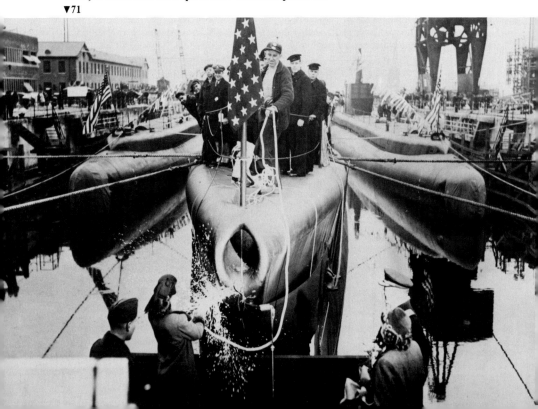

CHAPTER SIX

The Uncertain Offensive

I fear all we have done is to wake a sleeping giant and fill him with a terrible resolve. — Admiral Isoroku Yammamoto, Commander-in-Chief, Combined Fleet

The only thing now to do is to lick hell out of them. — Senator Burton K. Wheeler

T
WENTY-FIVE years later, across the other side of the world, a similar campaign was taking place with very different results. Japan, like Britain, was an island empire dependent on seaborne trade for the importation of food and raw materials. In the 1930s the Japanese military had embarked on an expansionist campaign in China which brought them into conflict with the Western powers, all of whom had considerable commercial interests in the area (which were more important than their oft-quoted concern for China's territorial integrity). The Japanese were aware that, sooner or later, they would very likely have to fight the United States, and their concern was to safeguard the natural resources of the area, particularly oil; this meant encroaching on the colonial territories of the European powers, particularly the Dutch East Indies with their vast mineral resources—a policy which became easier to execute as Europe became embroiled in the Second World War. However, Japanese expansionism was watched with growing unease by the United States and the result was an oil embargo imposed by the Americans in the summer of 1940, which only served to harden the Japanese in their determination to secure the natural resources of the region.

By the autumn of 1941 relations between the Japanese and the United States had deteriorated to the point where the Japanese leadership felt that, if conflict were inevitable, it had to seize the initiative from the start, cripple the US Pacific Fleet in a surprise attack and lay its hands on as much territory as possible. The result was the raid on Pearl Harbor on 7 December 1941. Thereafter the Japanese forces swept through the region. Malaya fell in February 1942, followed by the Philippines and the oil-rich Dutch East Indies. By April 1942 Japanese forces stood on the frontier of India and had secured the entire region. It is therefore somewhat ironic that, having gone to war in order to secure their mineral resources, the Japanese gave little thought to how their safe transport back to Japan could best be assured.

This neglect is hard to understand, for Japan had been Britain's ally in the First World War and her naval officers had seen for themselves how near to defeat Britain had come on account of the U-boat offensive. Moreover,

Japanese destroyers had deployed to the Mediterranean for convoy escort duties, and the officers in command of these ships had seen for themselves the efficacy of convoy. The answer lies in the traditions underpinning the relatively young Imperial Japanese Navy, the temperament of the Japanese naval officer, and a fundamental misunderstanding of the most likely enemy, the United States. In the Sino-Japanese War of 1894–95 and the Russo-Japanese War of 1904–05 the Japanese Navy had distinguished itself in fleet-to-fleet actions like the Battle of the Yalu River and the Battle of Tsushima. In the First World War the Japanese Navy's role was minimal; nevertheless, the Japanese naval officer concentrated his attention on the great fleet actions, such as Coronel, the Falklands, the Dogger Bank and Jutland.

The idea of a single, large, fleet-to-fleet action which would decide the war was summed up in the Japanese doctrine of *Kenteki Hissen*, or 'Fight the enemy on sight', which was drilled into cadets at Etajima, the Japanese naval academy. This doctrine suited the Japanese temperament. As Captain Atsushi Oi, one of the few Japanese naval officers to appreciate the importance of trade protection, wrote:

> Compared with the Europeans, the Japanese are generally said to be more impetuous and less tenacious. They prefer colourful and offensive fighting to monotonous and defensive warfare. It was only natural that convoy escorting and A/S warfare were not jobs welcomed by Japanese naval men.[1]

Other factors behind Japan's neglect of trade protection include the influence of the Nazi philosophy of autarky on the Japanese Government. Under an autarky there is little room for international trade, i.e. trade outside one's area of control. This sort of thinking led to a belief that the military conquest of an area automatically led to the complete economic control and exploitation of the resources of that area. In reality, however, no control can be so complete as to deny intrusion by enemy submarines.

Another factor in the IJN's unwillingness to study convoy protection is that many Japanese naval officer succumbed to the belief, widely held in inter-war naval and diplomatic circles, that unrestricted submarine warfare was underhand and criminal. The Japanese believed that the role of the submarine was to whittle down the enemy battle-fleet before the main engagement or finish off the cripples afterwards. They therefore assumed, with no supporting evidence, that the large American submarine force in the Pacific, together with the British 4th Submarine Flotilla in Chinese waters and any Dutch submarines in the East Indies, would be used solely against their battle-fleet. This was how the Japanese used their submarines, and as a result they missed one of their greatest opportunities of the war: the extended supply line from the West Coast of the USA was ignored—indeed, the Pacific

---

[1] A. Oi, *Why Japanese ASW Failed: The Japanese Navy in WW2 in the Eyes of Former Imperial Japanese Naval Officers* (Annapolis: US Naval Institute), p.359.

theatre was completely unmolested by Japanese submarines throughout the entire war.

If the Japanese Navy gave little thought to protecting its seaborne trade, then the Americans gave equally little thought to using their considerable submarine force in the Pacific against Japanese shipping. The order issued by the Chief of Naval Operations, Admiral Ernest King, on 7 December 1941 to 'execute unrestricted air and submarine warfare against Japan' came as something of a surprise. No such forthright order had ever been issued to a submarine force before. In December 1941 the United States had 51 submarines available for operations in the Pacific, 29 with the Asiatic Fleet based at Manila and 22 with the Pacific Fleet at Pearl Harbor. The submariners had been trained to fight a war of their own conception—a campaign against enemy warships, occasional surface engagements, tactical reconnaissance, minelaying. These were the roles that US submariners envisaged for themselves. The war they contemplated was an orthodox one in which the combatants observed the accepted rules of warfare defined by international agreement or custom.

Each US submarine was allocated a publication entitled *Instructions for the Navy of the United States Governing Maritime and Aerial Warfare*, which corresponded to the Prize Rules as defined in 1930 London Naval Treaty, for example:

> In their action with regard to merchant ships, submarines must conform to the rules of International Law to which surface vessels are subject.
> In particular, except in the case of persistent refusal to stop on being duly summoned, or active resistance to visit or search, a warship, whether surface vessel or submarine, may not sink or render incapable of navigation without having first placed passengers, crew and ship's papers in a place of safety.[2]

As the United States' relations with Japan deteriorated, this publication was studied assiduously by American naval officers who were taught to respect the written word. Submariners guilty of violating the rules would be 'hunted down, or captured and sunk as pirates'.[3]

Anger at the surprise attack on Pearl Harbor can be seen as one reason for the change in American policy, but the reality of the United States' situation was a more potent cause. It was military imperative which demanded recognition of the fact that military and economic power are inseparable: weakening the enemy's economic resources automatically weakens his war potential. With the best part of the US Pacific Fleet rendered *hors de combat* after Pearl Harbor, the submarines of the US Asiatic and Pacific Fleets were the only assets left to the Americans by which the war could be taken into the Japanese camp. As Theodore Roscoe, author of the official history of US submarine operations, wrote,

---

[2] T. Roscoe, *United States Submarine Operations in World War II* (Annapolis: US Naval Institute, 1949), p.18.
[3] *Ibid.*

There were to be no merchant ships in the Pacific for the duration of the war—cargo ships were merchantmen by genesis only. The US Navy was to consider all Japanese shipping as engaged in the prosecution of the war effort—either carrying men, munitions and equipment to areas under attack or occupation or freighting home the plundered raw materials from the conquered territory.

Armed or not, these merchant men were in effect combatant ships. 'Transports', 'freighters' and 'tankers' were hollow titles for auxiliaries of war, and it was the duty of the submarine force to reduce these ships to hulls as hollow as their titles. The polite little law book went overboard. Converted by a directive into commerce raiders, American submarines in the Pacific went to war to sink anything that floated under a Japanese flag.[4]

Soon after the attack on Pearl Harbor, half a dozen submarines of the US Pacific fleet sailed for patrols off Japan to implement this directive. The Asiatic Fleet submarines, driven from Manila by the seemingly unstoppable Japanese advance, were mainly engaged in operations in support of the US Army and it was not until they were able to establish bases in Western Australia that they were able to devote some attention to commerce raiding.

After the débâcle at Pearl Harbor and the rout in the Philippines, the twenty-five surviving submarines of the Asiatic Fleet withdrew to Fremantle in Western Australia. Five 'S' boats were sent round to Brisbane in Queensland, where they were joined by another five boats of the same class detached from the Pacific Fleet at Pearl Harbor. These boats were known as Task Force 42 (TF.42) under the command of Captain R. W. Christie, who was relieved on 23 November 1943 by Captain J. Fife. Fife would later assume command of all the Asiatic fleet boats. Their operational area was to be the Bismarck Sea, Solomons and New Guinea area. The twenty remaining fleet-type boats worked more distant areas around the Netherlands East Indies, the Phillipines and the South China Sea. They also worked the approaches to the ports of Manila, Davao, Surabaya, Singapore, Saigon and Cam Ranh Bay and the oil ports of Miri and Tarakan. Working these areas meant a round trip of some 6,600 miles to and from the patrol area, so a refuelling base was set up at Exmouth Gulf.

Patrols from Fremantle during April and May 1942 were neither profitable nor spectacular. A prime duty for all boats during this period was the evacuation of parties of stranded Europeans from various enemy-occupied islands. *Sturgeon*, *Skipjack*, *Salmon* and *Spearfish* were among the submarines which had successful patrols. *Spearfish* severely damaged the light cruiser *Naka* on 1 April while *Salmon* disposed of the 11,000-ton repair ship *Asahi* on 25 May.

By May 1942 sinkings had almost reached the 100,000-ton mark for the first time.[5] Ten of the sinkings were by Fremantle-based boats, and the number of successes would have been much higher but for certain factors.

---

[4]*Ibid.*, p.19.

There was an insufficient number of submarines effectively to block the trade routes between Japan and her empire. Areas such as the Makassar Strait, used by the Surabaya/Balik Papan tanker traffic to Truk, were often unpatrolled. Another factor was the inhibiting effect of pre-war training on submarine commanders when making attacks. They had been told to rely on their instruments and fire from a long range rather than get in close and use visual observation to sink the target. Commanding officers often kept their boats dived all day, even in areas of minimal Japanese air activity, they often waited for targets to come their way rather than seeking things out, they fired from extreme range and they dived deep out of trouble when threatened by a counter-attack. Diversions for special operations and rescue missions also meant that boats were taken away from commerce raiding. Overshadowing everything, however, was the dismal performance of American torpedoes—a major crisis which will be discussed in the next chapter.

When Lockwood relieved Wilkes on 26 May 1942 he set about examining the patrol reports of his commanding officers and was not pleased with what he found. Part of the blame could be laid on the faulty torpedoes but most American commanding officers did not seem to know what was required of them. Lockwood was ruthless. A patrol report which showed poor results would be followed by the commanding officer's immediate relief. *Snapper*'s commanding officer was relieved after his second patrol and his successor was himself relieved after *his* second patrol.

From May to August 1942 Asiatic Fleet submarines mounted twenty-eight patrols which produced a total of seventeen sinkings—a rate of little over half a ship per patrol. While the torpedo problem was one prime factor in the lack of success, poor management was another. Lockwood made no attempt to blockade the vital oil and raw material routes; instead, he followed the principle established by his predecessor, Wilkes, of stationing his boats at likely traffic points which 'Ultra' intercepts indicated would be used by Japanese shipping. It was 'catch as catch can', involving a considerable degree of wishful thinking.

Meanwhile the 'S' boats at Brisbane were not engaged in supporting the blockade at all: owing to the paucity of surface forces, they were wholly

---

[5]In considering the submarine campaign in the Pacific the writer is bedevilled by stastistics. In the following chapters two sets of figures have been used: first, from *Japanese Naval and Merchant Losses during World War II* produced by the US Joint Army Navy Committee (JANAC), and second, from *The Imperial Japanese Navy in WW2*, Japanese monograph No 116, prepared by the Military History Section, Special Staff, General Headquarters, Far East Command (former officers of the IJN) in February 1952. The JANAC list is a chronological record of all ships over 500grt which were sunk. The Japanese list is a similar document, but it includes vessels which were merely damaged. Owing to difficulties in translation, comparisons between the two lists are hard to make, and such a task is not made any easier by the Japanese custom of giving the same name to many ships of different tonnages and types (for example five *Takasago Marus* were sunk in May 1945 in various positions while the number of *Nanshin Marus* which became casualties runs to 35. The historian is also perplexed by the inability of the US authorities to agree upon a common figure. The US Strategic Bombing Survey (USSBS), in two reports, *The War Against Japanese Transportation* and *The Campaign of the Pacific War*, gives overall Japanese shipping losses as 8,141,591 tons and 8,515,277 tons respectively, while JANAC (Admiralty: Naval Staff History) quotes 8,618,109 tons. In the present work, figures have been taken from *The War Against Japanese Transportation*.

committed to supporting the US Army in the Solomons. There they had a thin time of it, for although the Japanese at this stage in the war had plenty of mercantile tonnage available, they used fast converted destroyers to run supplies in. The slow 'S' boats, lacking radar and equipped only with rudimentary attack instruments, found it hard to locate traffic and harder still to attack it. There was also the physical condition of these old boats' hulls, which were badly corroded and pitted, thus lessening their resistance to depth-charge attack. Habitability was unbelievably poor in the 'Pig Boats', which always had to remain dived all day when north of 15°. Consequently, from November 1942 they were withdrawn to the US for training duties, their place being taken by fleet boats detached from both Fremantle and Pearl Harbor.

The diversion of boats to the Solomons produced no improvement in results. From October to December 1942 twenty-four patrols were carried out from Brisbane yet only three achieved anything. Only six Japanese ships were sunk, two of them submarines. The problem was the same as that for the boats operating from Fremantle: they were being used reactively against Japanese shipping, constantly being shunted over the theatre in support of 'Ultra' information and being ordered against targets which were either heavily escorted or riding in well-protected anchorages under the protection of Japanese air cover. It is important to remember that at the time most Japanese tanker traffic was unescorted; a determined offensive would have hastened the end of the Solomons campaign considerably.

When the numbered fleet system was introduced into the US Navy in March 1943, the South West Pacific forces became known as the Seventh Fleet. At the same time the submarines on loan from the Pacific Fleet were withdrawn, leaving a force of twelve boats at Brisbane (TF.72) and eight (later increased to twelve) at Fremantle (TF.71).

In the campaign in the Upper Solomons, blockade duties often had to take second place to a variety of other tasks, including minelaying, surveying, the insertion and recovery of special forces and reconnaissance. However, with the successful conclusion of this campaign the need for 'Army co-operation' was dramatically reduced and in November 1943 the Brisbane boats were gradually transferred to Fremantle, from where they carried out patrols as far west as the Malay Barrier.

Unlike the Asiatic Fleet boats, the submarines of the Pacific Fleet where not required for operations in support of the Army and were deployed against Japanese commerce from the start. There were sixteen fleet-type boats (plus the five 'S' class transferred to Brisbane) under the command of Rear-Admiral T. Withers. Withers was succeeded on 14 May 1942 by Rear-Admiral R. H. English; he was killed in an air crash on 19 January 1943 and his place was filled by Lockwood. The names of Lockwood at Pearl Harbor and Christie and Fife at Fremantle would dominate the direction of the US submarine campaign.

The main base for the Pacific Fleet boats was Pearl Harbor. Limited repair facilities (for two boats only) were available at Midway Island which, however, could serve as a useful refuelling stop for boats going on and coming off patrol. The role of the Pacific Fleet boats was to establish a blockade around the islands of Japan together with the areas around the Marianas, the Marshall Islands, Truk and the Carolines. However, early experience showed that the patrols in the Mandated Areas and Truk would have to be abandoned in favour of the waters around Japan where traffic was dense, particularly around the southern ports of Yokohama and Nagasaki; the Mandated Territories and Truk would be left to boats newly arrived in the theatre and boats proceeding to and from Australia.

The distances travelled on the patrols on the Japanese Home Islands were immense. The average time on passage from Midway Island to Japan or Formosa was eight to twelve days, the submarine proceeding on the surface as long as the commanding officer deemed it safe. The submarine then remained on patrol for thirty days or until all her torpedoes had been expended. Thus a patrol could last sixty days if targets were scarce or thirty if the patrol was a profitable one. The average was about 48 days.

The first Pacific fleet boat to enjoy a successful patrol in Empire waters was *Trout* (Lt-Cdr Frank Fenno USN). The submarine departed from Pearl Harbor on 24 March 1942 and a fortnight later was off the south coast of Honshu. In a six-week patrol Fenno fired 22 of his 24 torpedoes, observed seven hits and sank three ships. Fenno attributed the relatively accident-free running of his torpedoes to the fact that they came from pre-war stocks at Pearl Harbor rather than subsequent issues.

Gudgeon, Triton, Drum, Tuna and *Pompano* also made relatively successful patrols during this period. *Gudgeon* and *Triton* both sank Japanese submarines—*I-173* and *I-164* respectively. However, the submarine game could be played by both sides, for *Thresher* was missed by three torpedoes fired from a submarine on 3 April 1942. On 1 May *Drum* disposed of the seaplane tender *Mizuho* off southern Japan. *Silversides* sank an auxiliary and a merchant ship off Honshu while *Greenling* had the unusual experience (for an American boat) of only needing one torpedo to dispatch the 3,200-ton *Kinjosan Maru*. The spring offensive for the boats of the Pacific Fleet ended with nineteen of the twenty-six boats being withdrawn from commerce raiding to support the Fleet at Midway and most of the others moved off station in a vain attempt to intercept the retiring Combined Fleet.

The transit route between Pearl Harbor and Australia could also prove profitable. *Tautog* (Cdr J. H. Willingham USN) sank a Japanese submarine (possibly *Ro-30*, though Japanese sources dispute this) on 26 April followed by another Japanese submarine, *I-28*, on 16 May. Willingham completed his transit by sinking the 4,467-ton *Shoka Maru* on 24 May. No wonder he was received in Australia with a hearty 'Well done!' from Admiral Lockwood. *Thresher* (Lt-Cdr William J. Millican USN), coming the other way during

July 1942, had a narrow escape when she was 'caught' by a Japanese grapple. After a tense period during which Millican ordered ciphers to be destroyed, *Thresher* eventually broke free. *Gudgeon* sank a 5,000-ton freighter while making the transit and damaged two others. Clearly, what Samuel Morrison referred to as the 'Pearl Harbor–Fremantle Shuttle' was an area full of useful targets.

But it was the waters around the Japanese Home Islands which proved to be the most lucrative area. By the summer of 1942 some boats were on their fourth or fifth patrols in the area. *Guardfish* (Lt-Cdr Thomas B. Klakring USN) had an encounter with a Japanese escort after an abortive attack (thanks to faulty torpedoes) on a transport on 19 August. Rather than accept the depth-charging which was his reward, he went after the destroyer. He missed, but his boldness later became doctrine: going after an escort was likely to be safer than waiting for a hammering. Klakring was an example of the new, young and aggressive submarine commander who was beginning to make an appearance in the Pacific. He was an engineering specialist who was once considered as being only a mildly promising officer. However, his first patrol proved that he had the determination to succeed. On 4 September 1942 he disposed of three ships totalling over 11,000 tons in daring and skilfully executed attacks close inshore. No one had sunk five ships on a patrol before, let alone three in a day. The successes were due to Klakring's placing his submarine in shallow water between the coast and the shipping lanes so that the attacks came from landward. For this patrol Klakring received a glowing endorsement from Rear-Admiral English and the Navy Cross.

The first year of the American offensive against shipping was a disappointment (see Table 9). Pacific-based submarines of the three commands (Pearl Harbor, Fremantle and Brisbane) had made about 350 patrols. They had been employed on coastal defence (around Lingayen and Midway), for blockade (Truk and the Solomons), for intercepting Japanese capital ships via 'Ultra' intercepts (which had proved totally unrewarding), for the interdiction of Japanese shipping, on a variety of special operations (largely in the Philippines), for delivering and evacuating personnel (Corregidor) and for general store carrying and weather forecasting in support of air strikes ('Doolittle Raid'). Seven boats were lost during 1942 (see below), so the Exchange Rate was one American submarine for every nineteen merchantmen—not a particularly healthy situation. In support of these operations seven boats had been lost, three 'S' boats (*S27*, *S36* and *S29*) by grounding, *Sealion* in the Japanese air raid on Cavite Navy Yard and three other boats (*Perch*, *Shark* and *Grunion*) to Japanese ASW measures.

Only one of these activities had done any real harm to Japan and the damage was, on the whole, negligible. This was the interdiction of Japanese merchant shipping. The three submarine commands had sunk 133 Japanese ships totalling 556,632 tons, equivalent to what 38 U-boats had sunk in the

TABLE 9: JAPANESE MERCHANTMEN SUNK BY US SUBMARINES, 1942[6]

Month	No of ships sunk	Tonnage	New Construction
January	7	28,351	
February	5	15,975	
March	7	26,183	
April	5	26,886	
May	20	86,110	
June	6	20,021	
July	8	39,356	
August	17½	76,632	
September	11	39,389	
October	25	118,920	
November	8	35,358	
December	14	43,171	
Total	133	556,352	260,059

Atlantic in February and March 1942. The campaign had not seriously interfered with the importation of raw material (coal, iron ore, bauxite, oil) for the 1942 figures was 20 million tons, very similar to that for 1941; moreover, the Japanese were actually able to increase the size of their tanker fleet, with new construction as well as with captured and salvaged tonnage. During the year Japan's total merchant tonnage fell by some 89,000 tons—a derisory figure.

The very considerable effort spent chasing Japanese capital ships as a result of 'Ultra' intercepts yielded very little in the way of results. Including the Battle of Midway and the Truk blockade, there were twenty-three sightings—five of battleships and eighteen of aircraft carriers. Four of the five contacts developed into attacks but only one battleship was damaged, a *Kongo* class vessel which was struck by a torpedo from *Flying Fish* (Lt-Cdr G. R. Donahoe USN). Ten of the eighteen aircraft carrier sightings developed into attacks but only three ships were damaged. Only two major units of the Japanese Fleet were sunk by US submarines, the cruiser *Kako* by the venerable *S44* and the light cruiser *Tenryu* by *Albacore*. In the war against Japanese submarines, US submarines sank six of the twenty-three boats lost.

By far the most successful US submarine operations were the fifty-four patrols conducted by the Pearl Harbor boats in the waters off Japan. These patrols, 15 per cent of the total number for 1942, accounted for eighty-one confirmed sinkings, or 45 per cent of the total. Had all the fleet boats been concentrated in these waters instead of fruitlessly chasing round the islands, then considerable inroads could have been made into Japan's merchant fleet.

The torpedo problem was a major cause of the lack of success. However, it is oversimplifying the matter to blame everything on the faulty Mk XIV torpedo and the Mk VI exploder. There was a failure of direction in US submarine strategy. The military and maritime theories of Clausewitz and

---

[6]Admiralty: Naval Staff History, *War with Japan, Vol. 5: The Blockade of Japan* (London, 1957), p.93. Also Roscoe, p.524.

Mahan were ignored. Instead of being directed against Japan's 'jugular vein', the submarines were shunted about the Pacific willy-nilly while the bulk of the Empire's shipping went about unescorted. Thus the evidence of the British experience during the Great War, which was reported in the Second World War off the American East Coast, was being ignored.

But future prospects were not altogether bleak. The problems with the torpedo were some way to being sorted out. A steady stream of new submarines was deploying to the Pacific, commanded by men like Klakring who had seen action as executive officers. The new submarines would be equipped with radar and a more powerful gun armament. The best hunting grounds were known, and there were plenty of commanding officers to take advantage of them.

One of the most remarkable aspects of the American armed forces during the Second World War is the speed with which they recovered from their initial defeats and dropped their peacetime attitudes. Time and time again, in Africa, in Italy, in the Atlantic, in France and in Germany, the forces of the United States would repay the Axis powers the lessons that they had learned the hard way. The year 1942 had been one of learning for the American submariners. They had taken some hard blows but they had benefited from them. The blockade of Japan was about to begin in earnest.

CHAPTER SEVEN

Two Constrasting Navies

*It was to the Submarine Force that I looked to carry the load until our great
industrial activity could produce the weapons we so sorely needed to carry the war to
the enemy.* — Fleet Admiral Chester W. Nimitz

*The Japanese were unable to grasp the importance of protecting their merchant
shipping or else they could not bring themselves to allocate first class material, either
ships or aircraft, for this purpose.* — Naval Staff History: The Blockade of Japan

NOTHING illustrates more the disparity between the Japanese and
the Americans during the Second World War than a comparison
between their tactics and equipment in the Pacific campaign against
commerce. On the one side the Americans exercised their industrial
capability to the full, so much so that by the middle of the war, construction
programmes were being scaled down. So great was the abundance of *matériel*
that submarines were being commissioned at a rate of almost five a month.
These submarines were equipped with the most up to date radar and had
levels of habitability undreamed of in other navies. On the other hand the
Japanese had refused to consider anti-submarine warfare in their pre-war
plans and as a result had to make do with vessels relegated from other duties
and crewed by officers and men considered not fit to serve with the
Combined Fleet. The Japanese Navy were the ultimate believers in the
Mahanian concept of the supremacy of the battle-fleet, and it is almost
impossible to exaggerate the hold which the battleships of the Combined
Fleet had over Japanese naval resources. Yet the Japanese were not without
some interesting ideas, and had these been properly developed and put into
widespread use then the American submariners might have had a very
different experience.

The United States Navy can be credited with commissioning the first
practical submarine into naval service. Yet the American Government had an
ambivalent attitude to submarine warfare, seeking at various times during the
inter-war period to abolish it or at the very least severely curtail submarine
operations. At the London Naval Conference in 1930 President Hoover had
declared that he was in favour of making ships carrying foodstuffs exempt
from submarine attack, conveniently forgetting that during the Civil War the
Union States had employed the blockade against the South to devastating
effect, stopping the supply of food and raw materials for which Hoover now
claimed freedom of movement.

Because their bases were few and widely scattered, the Americans
concentrated on the design of submarines which had considerable endurance,
good sea-keeping qualities and a high level of habitability. As a result,

American boats were considerably larger than contemporary British or German submarines. At the end of the First World War the most modern submarines in the US Fleet were the boats of the 'O', 'R' and 'S' classes which were of roughly 800–1,000 tons displacement and were armed with four 21in torpedo tubes. By the beginning of the Second World War the survivors of these classes had been relegated to training duties but in the early months of the war they were recalled to active service in the South-West Pacific area and around the Aleutians. These old boats had very low levels of habitability and in the extremes of climate in which they operated their crews had to endure conditions of some hardship.

However, during the 1920s and 1930s the 'Pig Boats' were gradually superseded by new classes of submarine which were a vast improvement. The boats which set the pattern for the US submarine construction in the inter-war period were the three *Barracuda* class submarines (for particulars of the *Barracuda* and other classes see Table 10), which were the first 'Fleet' submarines capable of cruising the vast distances required for operations in the Pacific. They were followed by the *Cachalot* class (two units), which introduced the all-welded hull into submarine service, then the five units of the 'P' class, the fifteen of the *Salmon* class and the nine of the 'T' class, which were the most modern boats in commission at the outbreak of war. These boats all had broadly similar characteristics: a long, sleek hull with a raked bow for good sea-keeping qualities, a substantial torpedo armament (though not as large as that of the British 'T' class with their ten 21in torpedo tubes) and a high standard of accommodation for the crew.

In addition to this line of development the US Navy commissioned the large minelaying submarine *Argonaut*, the large ocean-going boats *Nautilus* and *Narwhal* (based on the German U-cruisers of the Great War), the experimental *Dolphin* and the two boats of the 'M' class. The last three boats represented an unsuccessful attempt to incorporate the largest possible propulsion plant and armament into the smallest hull.

By far the largest number of American submarines in commission during the Second World War were the 195 units of the *Gato/Balao* classes. Following the experience gained with 'T' class, it was decided to commission

TABLE 10: PRINCIPLE PARTICULARS OF US SUBMARINES ENGAGED IN THE PACIFIC WAR

Class	Displacement (tons)	Armament	Complement
'S'	854/1,062	Four 21in tubes	42
Barracuda	2,000/2,620	Six 21in tubes, one 5in gun	80
Cachalot	1,210/1,650	Six 21in tubes, one 3in gun	50
'P'	1,310/1,960	Six 21in tubes, one 3in gun	55
Salmon	1,449/2,198	Eight 21in tubes, one 3in gun	70
'T'	1,475/2,370	Ten 21in tubes, one 3in gun	80–85
Gato/Balao	1,825/2,410	Ten 21in tubes, one 3in gun	60–80

six boats in the 1940 Programme, followed by a further 67 boats. These were to be broadly similar to the 'T' class but would incorporate differences in propulsion and external details. Their most noteworthy characteristics were good sea-keeping qualities, considerable endurance, a powerful armament and high standards of habitability. The hull, which was all-welded, was of considerable length (311ft) and of single form at the bow and stern but double amidships. The diesel-electric propulsion system consisted of four diesel engines coupled to four motors, linked in pairs to the shafts through reduction gears. This system offered considerable flexibility for surface operations because of the number of combinations which could be utilized and gave considerable power for high speed, surface cruising and battery charging.

While the last boats of the first series, the *Gato*s, were still building, a new series of 132 boats was ordered in the 1942 Programme. The *Balao* group were broadly similar to the *Gato*s but incorporated several design changes to allow more rapid construction using prefabricated sections. There were slight differences between boats built by different yards but, broadly speaking, all boats entering service between 1941 and 1944 were identical—something which helped to make the supply of spare parts easier for the maintenance and repair organizations. In general, the machinery in American boats worked well and there were few breakdowns, the exceptions being those fitted with HOR (Hoover-Owens-Rentschler) engines, which proved exceptionally unreliable in service. According to one commanding officer, Tommy Dykers of USS *Jack*, the HOR engine saved the Japanese 'thirty or forty ships'.[1] Following the *Gato/Balao* group were the *Tench* class, but only ten boats of the 146 hulls envisaged were completed in time to undertake a combat patrol. The *Tench* group were almost identical to the *Gato/Balao* group but were more strongly built and had a better internal layout.

During the war the surface armament of the *Gato/Balao* boats—and indeed that of the other classes—underwent considerable change. The first boats had a 3in 50-cal. gun and two 12.7mm machine guns. Later the calibre of the deck gun was increased to 4in in many boats and 20mm Oerlikons replaced the machine guns. The Oerlikons were not mounted on the conning tower but on sponsons fore and aft of it. From 1943 onwards many boats began to carry one, sometimes two, 5in guns specially adapted for submarine service. At the same time the 40mm Bofors gun, likewise in a specially adapted mounting, began to appear in US submarines, replacing or complementing the 20mm Oerlikons.

The gun armament of US submarines was superior to that of all other navies' boats. It was by no means unusual to see a boat armed with two 5in guns and a combination of 20mm Oerlikons and 40mm Bofors. The range of armament carried meant that there was a considerable variation in the size

---

[1]C. Blair, *Combat Patrol* (Bantam Books, 1978), p.191.

and shape of the conning towers of boats of this group. Normally there were two (though some boats carried three) periscopes, of considerable length and fitted with protective sleeves called 'shears', which doubled as useful perches for the lookouts.

From 1942 onwards American boats were fitted with a comprehensive radar outfit. At the beginning of the war many carried Type SD, an air-search radar which had, however, no offensive capabilities—it was purely a warning instrument. This was soon complemented by SJ, a surface-warning set which could locate and indicate directional bearing and the range of surface targets while the boat was dived. However, this set was unpopular with commanding officers in practice because in order to use it the boat had to run very shallow; moreover, control was difficult—the danger of broaching in full view of the enemy was ever present. In 1944 a periscope which included a built-in radar, ST, was introduced and dived attacks using radar became more practicable. One effect of the fitting of SJ was to increase the number of night attacks since Japanese ships did not zigzag at night and were thus easier to track.

With the benefit of a sophisticated radar outfit and the introduction of the PPI (Plan Position Indicator), a US submarine captain would adopt different tactics when attacking on the surface at night. Instead of taking his usual and traditional position on the bridge, he would conduct the attack from the conning tower, where the PPI would give him a far better picture of the situation than the sharpest night vision ever could. Thus many commanding officers were now able to resist the tendency to fire at too great a range which resulted from the optional illusions created by night vision (objects look closer at night than they do in daytime).

The habitability of American boats was of considerable concern to their designers and in this respect, as in so many others, American boats were far ahead of those in other navies. American submariners had the best of everything and would not have tolerated the squalid conditions taken for granted by others. However, in some boats what one author has described as a 'frontiersman attitude to life below to emphasise its ruggedness' pertained. Beards were unnecessary since the Kleinschmidt distillers produced seven hundred gallons of water daily and US submariners were never short of water; in some boats a washing machine was installed and it was possible for the crew to have clean clothes throughout a long patrol. Efficient air-conditioning not only removed the stench of oil, food and humanity which was the norm in most submarines but kept the boats free from damp, thus reducing the number of electrical failures. Habitability and good engineering practice went hand in hand.

American attention to detail was comprehensive. The complicated heads (toilets) which were blown direct into the sea with the attendant risk of 'getting your own back' common in other navies were not fitted in American boats. Instead the heads drained down into one tank which was discharged when operationally convenient. It did not always work: in USS *Hawkbill* on one occasion, sea pressure lifted the relief valve and the tank vented inboard with potentially catastrophic results until Ensign Rex Murphy who, showing a courage surely beyond the call of duty, waded into the 'miasmic fog' and held the valve shut for an hour until it could be fixed.

The health of the crew was catered for while on patrol by a properly qualified Pharmacist's Mate and thus the men did not have to suffer the amateur attentions of the commanding officer or coxswain as in other navies. Pharmacists' Mates were more than qualified to deal with the kind of ailments that cropped up on patrol, though some exceeded their brief considerably. On board USS *Seadragon* (Lt-Cdr Ferrsall) on 11 September 1942, for example, Corpsman Wheeler B. Lipes performed an appendectomy on Seaman Darrell Rector who had collapsed. Lt Noreel Ward acted as Lipes' assistant while the Communications Officer, Lt Franz Hoskins, acted as anaesthetist and the Engineer Officer, Lt Charles Manning, doubled as chief nurse. While Ferrsall kept the boat steady in a quiet area, Lipes got on with the job on the wardroom table. Similar operations happened on board *Grayback* and *Silversides* before the doctors stepped in to stop what was described as an 'undesirable medical practice'.[2]

However, the Achilles' heel of the American submarine service was its torpedoes. At one stage the torpedo problem amounted to nothing less than a crisis of confidence in their equipment among US submarine commanders on the one hand and in the commanders among the staff on the other. From the beginning of the war, patrol reports were received which contained records of the target being missed even through the torpedo was running 'hot, straight and normal'. The torpedoes most widely used by the US submarine force were the Mk 10 for the 'S' class and the Mk 14 for the fleet boats.

The 21in Mk 10 was a veteran over ten years old. It weighed 2,215lb and had a range of 32,500yds at a speed of 36kts, with a warhead of 497lb of TNT or 485lb of Torpex. The Mk 3 exploder with which it was fitted was a simple device designed to detonate the warhead on contact with the target. The Mk 14 was a much larger weapon, weighing 3,280lb and with a range of 4,500yds at 45kts or 9,000yds at 36kts. The warhead was 635lb of Torpex. The torpedo was fitted with the Mk 6 exploder, an extremely complicated mechanism which was designed to explode on impact with the target but also incorporated a magnetic setting that would detonate the warhead when the torpedo passed through the magnetic field under or around the target. It had been designed by the Naval Torpedo Station at Newport, Rhode Island, but under such conditions of secrecy that at the time of Pearl Harbor only commanding officers and their torpedo officers were authorized to know of its existence.

The first problem to occur was in reports from commanding officers that

---

[2] R. Compton-Hall, *The Underwater War* (Blandford Books, 1982), p.37.

their torpedoes appeared to be running at depths greater than those set. Lt-Cdr Tyrell Jacobs of *Sargo*, a torpedo specialist, fired thirteen torpedoes in December 1941 without a single hit. He reasonably concluded that either the torpedo was running deep or the Mk 6 exploder was faulty—or both. He was rewarded by Captain Wilkes with a reprimand and a refusal to carry out simple tests. Jacobs was not alone: submarine patrol reports for the first six months of 1942 are packed with references to errant torpedo running.

The policy of blaming commanding officers for torpedo failures continued and in cases may have been right. Commanding officers had faith in the torpedo data computer and its gyro angle transmitter, which were outstanding control instruments. However, these machines were so sensitive that the slightest slip in operating would ruin the attack and with the huge expansion of the submarine force it is unquestionable that mistakes did occur. Until Rear Admiral Charles Lockwood became ComSubAsiatic in April 1942, commanding officers had to endure the indifference of higher command. However, Lockwood took note of their complaints and shortly after assuming his appointment he received a memorandum from Lt-Cdr John Coe of *Skipjack* which minutely analysed his torpedo performance during his last patrol and concluded:

> To make an 8,500 mile round trip into enemy waters, to gain attack position undetected within 800 yards of enemy ships only to find that the torpedoes run and over half the time fail to explode, seems to me to be an undesirable manner of gaining information which might be determined any morning within a few miles of any torpedo station in the presence of comparatively few hazards.[3]

Lockwood decided to take the matter further and did so both through official channels, by formally enquiring of the Bureau of Ordnance whether there was any evidence of deep running in the Mk 14 or defects in the Mk 6 exploder, and by writing a personal letter to Admiral Richard Edwards, personal assistant to the formidable Admiral Ernest J. King, Chief of Naval Operations. He received a frosty response from the Bureau of Ordnance, which blamed poor torpedo performance on incompetent commanding officers. Consequently, taking matters into his own hands Lockwood set up his own tests at Frenchman's Bay near Fremantle, using Coe's *Skipjack*. The results were astonishing: after a series of trial runs it was found that, on average, a Mk 14 ran 11ft deeper than set. On 22 June Lockwood sent his results to the Bureau. At Pearl Harbor Bob English saw Lockwood's message, which was sent only four days after English had listed eight reasons for torpedo failure, most of which related to errors by commanding officers and crews. He now did a complete *volte-face* and enquired of the Bureau whether any reports of deep running had been received.

But the Bureau were not so easily convinced. They rejected the results of the *Skipjack* tests as 'unscientific'. Lockwood was furious and repeated the

---

[3]Blair, p.56.

tests using *Saury*, with the same results—the torpedoes ran an average of 11ft deeper than set. This time Lockwood's submission had a result. Admiral King, who, as CNO, would have been aware of Lockwood's concern, ordered the Bureau of Ordnance to get to the root of the matter. Consequently the Bureau, using the submarine *Herring*, ran a series of trials which produced the result that the Mk 14 ran on average 10ft deeper than set. On 1 August 1942, almost eight months after the attack on Pearl Harbor, the Bureau conceded that the Mk 14 had been improperly tested and that it ran approximately 10ft deeper than set and issued the appropriate instructions on how to make the necessary modifications.

This was the first victory for the submariners but they were not totally satisfied. Many still felt that the Mk 6 exploder was unreliable. Yet they had a hard time convincing Lockwood and English. Both commanders felt that, since the torpedoes had been running too deep, the exploders had been outside the target's magnetic field, which was why they failed to detonate. Now that the depth-keeping problem had been remedied, the magnetic exploder would work. Here Lockwood and English were disregarding British experience with their CCR pistol which had failed to operate and the German Navy's experience with a similar device.

However, solving the depth-keeping problem only seemed to increase the incidence of torpedoes exploding prematurely or not exploding at all, despite having run true and in some cases having been heard to strike the target. *Tunny* (Lt-Cdr J. A. Scott), on her first patrol on 8 February 1943, fired two torpedoes at the 5,306-ton *Kusuyama Maru* at the southern end of the Formosa Strait. The first ran wild and the second was not heard by *Tunny*'s sonar operators so probably sank. Under fire from the freighter, *Tunny* launched two more, one of which circled; the other made a straight run but failed to explode. Still under fire, *Tunny* fired a further three torpedoes: the first hit, the second missed and the third, after zigzagging down the track, also hit the target, which sank in twenty minutes. That episode at least had a more satisfactory ending than *Tunny*'s attack on a carrier task force south-west of Truk in the night of 9–10 April. At a range of 800yds the submarine fired her stern tubes at *Taiyo*, followed by her six bow tubes at *Hiyo* only 600yds away. Seven explosions were heard but only *Taiyo* was hit by a single torpedo. On 11 June 1943 *Trigger* (Lt-Cdr Roy Benson) fired six torpedoes at *Hiyo* in Tokyo Bay. Four explosions were heard and claimed as such by *Trigger*'s commanding officer on his return from patrol. Lockwood, however, knew differently: 'Ultra' intercepts told him that *Hiyo* had been hit by one torpedo which had barely damaged her. *Sargo* had a string of thirteen consecutive misses and *Seadragon* had fifteen.

While the controversy over the torpedoes was going on, Lockwood had taken over at Pearl Harbor from Rear Admiral English, who had been killed in a plane crash. Lockwood's replacement at Fremantle was Captain Ralph Christie, whose appointment introduced a new element into the torpedo question. Christie was a torpedo specialist who had had a considerable part in the design of the Mk 6 exploder and whose personal prestige was thus at stake in the controversy.

Trigger's failure to sink *Hiyo* finally persuaded Lockwood to order his commanding officers to deactivate the magnetic settings on the Mk 6. This he was able to do on 24 June 1943 by direct order of Admiral Nimitz. But down in Fremantle Christie chose to ignore Lockwood's action, which he could get away with since he came under the command of General Douglas MacArthur. This divergence in opinion placed US submarine commanders in a quandary: when they worked for Lockwood they deactivated their magnetic exploders but as soon as they passed under Christie's command they had to activate them once more. Christie was unrepentant in his support for the Mk 6. Lt-Cdr 'Red' Ramage of USS *Trout* told Christie that 'If I get 25 per cent reliability from your torpedoes I'll be lucky', while Lt-Cdr 'Moke' Millican of USS *Thresher* complained that after an attack on a Japanese submarine his torpedo had merely 'clinked 'em with a clunk'. Millican's reward was to be relieved of his command and sent back to the USA for a rest and an appointment to a new construction. However, all was still not well with the Mk 6. Lockwood's commanding officers, now using the contact setting on the exploder, found that torpedoes were failing to explode after apparently running true. Even the Japanese noticed that merchant ships were coming back into harbour with US torpedoes lodged intact in their sides.

The ultimate story of US torpedo failure concerns *Tinosa*'s (Lt-Cdr Dan Daspit) attack on the 19,000-ton whale factory ship *Tonan Maru* on 24 July 1943. This story has been oft-told before but loses none of its relevance as an example for that. Daspit, by all accounts an exceptionally skilled attacker, found the *Tonan Maru* on the morning of 24 July and made an 'end around' to dive ahead of the target. He attacked, fired four torpedoes and saw two of them hit forward but to no apparent effect. He fired two more: both hit, one aft which caused smoke. The target began to settle by the stern but showed no sign of sinking. Daspit recorded what happened next in his patrol report:

1009	Having observed target carefully and found no evidence of a sinking, approached and fired one torpedo at starboard side. Hit, heard by sound to stop at the same time. I observed large splash. No apparent effect. Target had corrected list and was firing at periscope and at torpedo wakes with machine guns and one inch [gun].
1011	Fired eighth torpedo. Hit. No apparent effect.
1014	Fired ninth torpedo. Hit. No apparent effect. Target firing at periscope when exposed and at torpedo tracks when running.
1039	Fired tenth torpedo. Hit. No apparent effect.
1048	Fired eleventh torpedo. Hit. No apparent effect. This torpedo hit well aft on the port side, made a splash at the side of the ship and was then observed to have taken a right turn and to jump clear of the

	water about one hundred feet from the stern of the vessel. I find it hard to convince myself that I saw this.
1050	Fired twelfth torpedo. No effect.
1100	Fired thirteenth torpedo. Hit. No effect. Circled again to fire at other side.
1122	Picked up high speed screws.
1125	Sighted destroyer approaching from the east.
1131	Fired fourteenth torpedo. Hit. No effect.
1132½	Fired fifteenth torpedo. Started deep. Destroyer range 1,000 yards. Torpedo heard to hit tanker and stop running by sound. Periscope had gone under by this time. No explosion. Had already decided to retain one torpedo for examination by base.[4]

What the crew of the *Tonan Maru* made of all this has not been recorded.

When Daspit returned to Pearl Harbor and reported to Lockwood, the latter decided to dispense with further dispatches to the Bureau of Ordnance and deal with the problem himself. Lockwood ordered a firing trial from *Muskallunge* against the submerged cliffs at Kahoolawe. When one of the torpedoes failed to go off after hitting the cliffs it was, gingerly, recovered for examination. It was found from this, and from subsequent trials which included dropping a torpedo nose-first from a dockyard crane, that when the warhead hit the target at a angle of 90 degrees the exploder mechanism was crushed before it could set off the charge; when the warhead hit the target at 45° only about half the torpedoes failed to go off.

While the experts at Pearl Harbor worked on means of correcting this problem, commanding officers at sea were ordered to use as fine an angle as possible when attacking the target—which went against everything that had been taught to do. Eventually the firing pin of the exploder was reduced in weight so that it took up less friction on the guide studs. This was a modification which could easily be carried out in the machine shops at Pearl Harbor. On 30 September 1943 USS *Barb* left Pearl Harbor with an outfit of twenty torpedoes, each equipped with the new firing pin:

> The Gordian Knot had been cut and the faulty exploder had been corrected. At last, almost two years after the beginning of the war, US submarines went to sea with a reliable torpedo.[5]

Alas, problems with torpedoes were still with the submariners, though not on the scale experienced before. The Mk 18 electric torpedo, introduced in January 1944, caused endless trouble:

---

[4]Blair, p.179.

[5]T. Roscoe, *United States Submarine Operations in World War II* (Annapolis: US Naval Institute, 1949), p.261.

The first ones taken to sea lacked hydrogen burning circuits and therefore had to be frequently withdrawn from the tubes for ventilation. Several instances of hydrogen explosions and fires occurred. One fire on board the *Flying Fish* heated the warhead until the Torpex melted and ran. There were some erratic runners, slow runners and sinkers. The torpedoes' tail vanes were found to be weak and had to be strengthened. Cold water and low battery temperature caused the torpedo to run slow and several misses were due to this to this unforeseen obstacle. Hot runs in the tubes following depth charging were caused by the failure of the guide studs. Warping of the thin shell of the battery compartment resulted in binding in the tubes.[6]

Worst of all, one errant Mk 18 came round and sank the submarine that fired it: USS *Tang* was sunk by one of her own torpedoes in the Formosa Strait on 25 October 1944.

The torpedo problem was the one serious setback for the US submarine force during the Second World War. It weakened the confidence of the staff in the submarine commanders and vice versa. It undoubtedly prolonged the submarine campaign since many targets escaped which otherwise would have gone to the bottom. However, once it had been solved, the submariners could get on with the job.

When considering American forces in the Pacific, the logistics side must not be forgotten. None of the belligerents in the Second World War excelled in logistics like the Americans. Their submariners wanted for nothing despite the fact that all their food, stores, weapons, fuel and all the other impedimenta with which the United States goes to war had to come by sea across the Pacific. At the various bases were skilled repair teams, while the Submarine Operational Research Group (SORG) saw that each commanding officer's patrol report was minutely analysed to provide information concerning machinery and weapon performance, tactics, optimum firing ranges and a host of other details vital to the successful prosecution of the war. The totality of the American effort was stupendous.

Lastly, the Americans' use of signals intelligence must be taken into account. Breaking the Japanese codes gave them priceless information which could be used against the enemy. However, it could, and sometimes did, lead to a fondness for over-centralized control by the force commanders, boats being sent off in search of specific contacts discovered through signals intelligence. Such hunts were not always successful.

The problems which the Americans had with their torpedoes and their HOR engines pale into insignificance when considering the Japanese anti-submarine force, its tactics and its weapons. Since the Japanese considered that the main function of the submarine was to attack the enemy battle-fleet, they made few preparations for anti-submarine warfare other than screening their fleet. At the outbreak of war, to protect their merchant shipping they had allocated no more than 200 vessels—ten destroyers and destroyer escorts,

---

[6]Roscoe, p.262.

TABLE 11: KAIBOKAN CONSTRUCTION

Type	Standard displacement (tons)	Speed (kts)	Armament
A (*Shimushu*)	860	19.7	Three 12cm guns, fifteen 25mm machine guns
B (*Mikura*)	940	19.5	Two 12cm DP guns, fifteen 25mm machine guns
C (even-numbered)	745	16.5	Two 12cm DP guns, fifteen 25mm machine guns
D (odd-numbered)	740	17.5	Two 12cm DP guns, fifteen 25mm machine guns

eight torpedo boats, 55 submarine-chasers, 42 gunboats, 92 minesweepers, six minelayers and a few miscellaneous craft. Even as late as August 1944 the total had increased to no more than 274—10 per cent of the optimum requirement—of which only 60 were long-range vessels.

A class of frigates known as *Kaibokan* were ordered late in the war and it was hoped to build 263, with 190 being constructed in the year 1944–45. In the event, only 167 were commissioned, in four sub-groups (see Table 11). They carried a small number of depth charges to begin with, twelve, but this later increased to 130. The Japanese also constructed a considerable number of small, slow, wooden submarine-chasers ('SCS' class) and a larger class of submarine-chasers ('PC' class) which were 167ft long, carried thirty-six depth charges and were fitted with an 8cm gun and a twin 13mm machine gun. In general, Japanese escorts varied from old, converted stock armed with inadequate equipment to new ships armed with the best that the Japanese could provide. These latter ships were dangerous hunters of submarines. The destroyer which sank the British submarine *Stratagem* on 22 November 1944 in the Strait of Malacca in a snap depth-charge attack in shallow water was no amateur at the ASW game.

The Japanese did resort to using Q-ships, one such being sunk off the north coast of Java on 22 January 1945 by HMS *Spark*. An interesting variant on the Q-ship theme was to station soldiers in the holds of craft likely to be boarded by a party from an Allied submarne. HMS *Trenchant*'s boarding officer came face to face with an armed Japanese soldier when boarding a schooner in the Celebes on 13 July 1945. He hurriedly withdrew as the Japanese party opened fire. *Trenchant* then sank the schooner by gunfire. In view of this and two previous incidents, Admiral Fife ordered submariners to be extremely wary when approaching any small craft.

The standard Japanese depth charge contained about 230lb of explosive. Anti-submarine bombs carried by aircraft were 131lb and 550lb, the latter being preferred when available. The Japanese had no means of determining the depth of a submarine under attack and so a pattern of depth charges was usually dropped with a variety of settings on the time fuze (hydrostatic fuzes were unavailable). Early experience in the war showed that the settings were insufficiently deep, but in the autumn of 1942 they were radically modified, possibly as a result of loose talk in the US press. No ahead-throwing weapons were produced by the Japanese during the war.

Until the General Escort Command was formed in November 1943, escorts and other ASW craft were divided amongst the nine naval 'districts' around the Home Islands and the Northern Force covering the island of Hokkaido and the Kuriles. Outside the Home Islands, escorts came under the orders of the local commander or those of the China Area Fleet. Each commander was responsible for the shipping in his own area and often his instructions came direct from the naval staff in Tokyo. This resulted in huge variations in operational practice and efficiency. Exchange of information regarding arrivals and departures of merchant ships and the movements of enemy submarines was inadequate, and the procedure for co-ordinating shipping was very loose. The Japanese evinced an extraordinary lack of interest in the progress and conduct of the war outside their own immediate sector.

The Japanese were temperamentally unsuited to ASW. When prosecuting a contact they all too readily gave up on the flimsiest of evidence of a sinking despite knowing of the deceptive practices of their own submariners. Later on in the war, greater persistence in attack was urged until definite confirmation of a kill was found. Even so, the longest hunt carried out by a Japanese escort during the war lasted only 31 hours.

At the start of the war the asdic devices of the IJN were well up to the standard of the day. Considering their current dominance of the world electronics industry, it is strange to reflect that during the war the Japanese failed to keep up with other navies and as late as 1943 the main method of attack used against submarines was to run down the track of the torpedo, drop a pattern of depth charges, then listen. Officers were not familiar with the properties of sound transmission underwater and no tactical use was made of such information. Escorts were not fitted with bathythermographs and there was little understanding of density layers at sea and their influence on submarine operations. Moreover, there was little attempt to make the disposition of the convoy escort conform with the effective sonar range for the locality. The disposition of escorts at ranges of 1,000 to 2,000 metres from the convoy reflected the Japanese belief that this was the range from which an Allied submarine would deliver an attack. American submariners soon had the measure of Japanese ASW practice and were able to circumvent any screen with ease. It is true that after the war the various Allied naval missions found that a great deal of research into ASW techniques and weapons was being done in Japan. However, the gap between these ideas and their concrete expression was immense.

Air cover for convoys was provided by small groups of between six and twenty seaplanes assigned to each naval district. The air training groups were also available to assist in ASW operations if required. In the more distant areas of the Empire, air cover was provided by land-based naval air flotillas, of which three were in existence on the outbreak of war and a further fifteen commissioned during hostilities. After 1943 the Japanese became more impressed with the value of air escorts for convoys (as the British in two world wars had been before them) and, particularly in the South China Sea, air escorts were increased and Army air personnel co-opted to assist in convoy protection. Five escort carriers were allocated for convoy protection work but never operated as such. The demands of the Combined Fleet came first and the ships were continually employed with the fleet or on ferry operations. Long-range, land-based aircraft gave distant cover over the convoy routes and on 'sweeping' duties off the principle anchorages. However, there was no organization such as the RAF's Coastal Command to co-ordinate air–sea operations.

Communications between ships and aircraft were bad and messages often had to be routed through a shore station. It was almost certainly due to poor communications that only one hunting group of esorts with attached air cover was formed, and this was late in 1945. It consisted of five *Kaibokan* organized as the 102nd Squadron with twenty naval fighters from the 934th Air Force at Shanghai. The aircraft were equipped with radar and MAD (see later) and modified to carry depth charges. Searches were co-ordinated by the escort commander, the method being to send a couple of the frigates on a sweep between Shanghai and Formosa with aircraft doing MAD and radar sweeps over the same area. Any MAD/radar contacts would be followed up either by the aircraft or by the *Kaibokan* and, it was hoped, depth-charged to destruction. The hunting group made no kills.

Japanese radar was in its infancy at the beginning of the war although it is reported that British *matériel* found at Singapore greatly assisted the Japanese with their own research. From November 1943 some escorts began to receive an air-warning set; however, a proper surface-search set was not developed. Passive measures such as homing in on the radar beam from an Allied submarine were used—British submariners were warned that their Type 291 transmissions could be detected—but in terms of detecting targets the Japanese Navy still relied on the 'Mark 1 eyeball' more than anything else.

The Japanese began to experiment with radar countermeasures as early as 1943. These included the use of decoys, 'Window' and airborne jamming devices. However, one interesting Japanese development was the use of the Magnetic Airborne Detector (now better known as the Magnetic Anomaly Detector) or MAD. This equipment detected variations in the Earth's magnetic field caused by large metal objects such as submarines and some 200 Japanese aircraft were eventually fitted with it. The instrument had an average range of 150 metres but could reach as far as 250 metres under ideal conditions. To be effective the pilot had to fly at a height of between 10 and 50 metres above sea level. MAD-equipped aircraft were employed to sweep ahead of convoys, and it was estimated that a six-plane MAD sweep gave 100 per cent coverage ahead of a 10kt convoy; using three aircraft, sweeping was

60 per cent effective. The Japanese claimed that seven Allied submarines were sunk as a result of MAD attacks, four in the Home Islands area and three in the South Seas. Since no more than fifteen Allied submarines in all were lost (including the Dutch *O19*, by grounding) during the twelve months that MAD was in use, this claim should be treated with considerable reserve.

In short, when set against the huge material resources of the United States with its seemingly unending supplies of high-quality equipment, the Japanese effort can be summed up as 'too little, too late'.

CHAPTER EIGHT

Defending the Empire's Sea Lanes

Their lack of practice will make them unskilled and their lack of skill will make them timid in battle. — Pericles

In a nutshell, Japan failed in ASW because her Navy disregarded the importance of the problem. — Captain Atsushi Oi, IJN

I N 1941 JAPAN went to war with her Navy obsessed with the battle-fleet ('Combined Fleet' in Japanese naval parlance) and with her supply lines left totally unprotected. Her economic position consisted of a number of imponderables. Though an industrial power, she lacked the economic muscle for a long war. She could deliver one tremendous blow, and thereafter little. Moreover, she was heavily dependent on outside sources for the supply of food and raw materials. Most of her imports came from an area known as the Inner Zone, which comprised Japan (the Home Islands), Korea, Manchuria, Formosa, Karafuto and North China. However, all her petrol and rubber, certain metals and 20 per cent of her iron ore came from the Outer Zone which comprised Japan's mandated islands (former German territories ceded to Japan under League of Nations Mandates after the Great War) and from her conquests early in the Second World War. But it was a source of weakness that this vital region was connected by a long and inherently vulnerable line of communications with the Home Islands, where the country's entire industrial potential was situated.

In this respect, Japan's merchant marine was her Achilles' heel. Before the war merchant ship construction was neglected in favour of warship construction. China and Russia were seen as potential enemies, so the Naval Estimates were always under pressure from the Army. Consequently merchant shipping construction enjoyed a diminishing share of a diminishing cake. Japan began the war with 2,528 merchant ships of 6,337,000 gross tonnage. Of these, 1,528 ships (2,436,000grt) were allocated for civilian use, 519 (2,160,500grt) for the Army and the remainder, 482 ships (1,740,200grt), for the Navy. The possibility of wartime losses was not seen as serious: annual losses amounting to between 800,000 and 1,000,000 tons gross were predicted, but new construction at 600,000 tons annually would compensate adequately for those. By April 1942 some 3,000,000 tons of shipping allocated to the services was scheduled to be returned to civilian use, but over-ambitious plans for further conquests, followed by some unexpected defeats, meant that the majority of the ships were retained by the military.

In the meantime Japan neglected every form of commerce protection. No department within the Navy Ministry was responsible for this aspect of Japan's war effort. While there were ten officers on the Naval Staff concerned with operations (i.e. Combined Fleet operations) there were four concerned with what were euphemistically known as 'Rear Echelon' matters, including convoy protection. There was one officer responsible for ASW before the war. After Pearl Harbor another was appointed to share the work load, and one was then responsible for mining and AA defence while the other dealt with commerce protection.

At the same time every Japanese base, regardless of size, considered its main priority to be the support of the Combined Fleet. At Yokosuka, an important base responsible for some 600 miles of eastern coastline along the island of Honshu and the important sea route to Iwo Jima, there was one officer responsible for trade protection and his duties also included education and training. At sea, troopships were always accompanied by an escort detached from the Combined Fleet. The remainder of Japan's merchant traffic was encouraged to proceed independently, in order to speed up the turn-around time of shipping in loading or discharging cargo. Strangely enough, regulations for the control of shipping did exist but they differed from region to region and depended on the enthusiasm, or otherwise, of the local commander.

Another problem faced by the Japanese was the extended and difficult nature of their lines of communications. Two main routes went out from Japan to her overseas conquests. One ran to the Philippines, Singapore and ultimately Burma while the other went to New Guinea and Rabaul and eventually to Guadalcanal in the Solomons. These routes were like the two sides of a triangle with Japan at the apex. The pattern of shipping movements was for vessels to sail up and down these sides—which was a gross under-exploitation of assets. The Japanese were never able to organize the middle passage across the 'base' of the triangle.

Despite their early successes in the war, by the middle of 1942 the Japanese were beginning to suffer from the shipping losses caused by US submarines. Consequently, on 10 April 1942 the First and Second Escort Groups were formed and a very limited form of convoy introduced. The First Escort Group, consisting of ten old destroyers, two torpedo boats and five converted gunboats, was to escort traffic between Singapore and Moji in Japan. The Second Escort Group, consisting of four destroyers, two torpedo boats and a gunboat, worked the important 3,000-mile route between the Home Islands and the base at Truk in the Carolines. It is not surprising that the convoys covered by these small forces were small and organized according to the whims of local commanders.

By the middle of 1942 the Japanese had suffered their first reverse at the Battle of the Coral Sea, and this was swiftly followed by the disaster which overtook them at Midway. At the same time shipping losses due to submarine attack were also rising, particularly in the East China Sea. In response to this situation the First Convoy Escort Fleet was created in June 1942 under the command of Admiral T. Nakajima, who had his headquarters on the island of Formosa and was responsible for the organization and protection of convoys in the East China Sea. Later his area was extended to cover the Japan–Palau route, and officers from Nakajima's staff were appointed to existing IJN commands in Moji, Singapore, Saigon and Manila. However, the resources allocated to Nakajima were barely equal to the task: all he had was eight superannuated destroyers. If the ships were old, then so were the men. Nakajima was an officer brought out of retirement and many of his colleagues either were considered unfit for appointments in the Combined Fleet or were reservists. The escort captains were competent seamen but were limited in their outlook and not receptive to new ideas. (A similar situation existed in the Royal Navy during the Second World War between officers in the Home Fleet and those in the Western Approaches Command.)

Nevertheless Nakajima did his best. Convoys usually consisted of six to eight ships escorted by one destroyer. He instituted pre-sailing conferences which would be attended by the Masters of the merchant ships, the escort commander, the convoy commodore and a respresentative from the staff of the First Convoy Escort Fleet. But he met with considerable hostility and a lack of co-operation from officers of the Combined Fleet. Combined Fleet warships proceeding to or from the Home Islands would sail independently when they could have easily escorted a convoy for all or part of their voyage. The excuse preferred by the Combined Fleet Staff was that trade protection could not be allowed to interfere with Fleet movements.

In October 1942 convoy took another step forward with the formation of an independent division within the *Gunreibu* (Naval General Staff) dealing with protection of shipping. Known as the Twelfth Division of the First Bureau, this was headed by a captain supported by three staff officers. One was responsible for homeland defence, the second for convoys, routeing and ASW in general and the third for the defensive arming of merchantmen. It was a start, but it was still very small beer compared with the massed ranks of staff officers in the gunnery and naval aviation sections of the naval staff. At about the same time there was some attempt to standardize the haphazard local arrangements which existed for the protection of shipping by the promulgation of a directive entitled 'The Doctrines concerning the Protection of Sea Communications during the Greater East Asia War'.

The introduction of these measures, together with the addition to Japan's merchant fleet of captured shipping and new construction (not forgetting the problems American submariners were experiencing with their torpedoes), meant that the Japanese merchant marine was at its healthiest in August 1942. Some shipping could be released to civil control and the civil tonnage rose to over 3,000,000grt as a result. Despite wartime losses, the overall tonnage available, 6,266,800grt, was only a few thousand tons less than the total at the outbreak of the war. But in August 1942 the Americans launched their assault on the island of Guadalcanal, which lasted until January 1943. By then the American submarine blockade was beginning to bite. Major Y. Horie, an army liaison officer at First Convoy Fleet HQ, wrote in his diary:

> The news was bad from every direction. There were shortages of ammunition in New Guinea, shortages of both petrol and gasoline in Truk and Japan, insufficient bauxite at every plant, shortage of escort ships and shortage of ships to be escorted. Pleas [for more escort ships and anti-aircraft guns] came into Tokyo in an unending stream. An atmosphere of gloom descended on Imperial General Headquarters. Such was the shortage of escorts that on one occasion, thirty-two ships in Palau harbour waited ninety-five days for lack of one escort ship to travel back to the Japanese home ports with them.[1]

In March 1943 a Second Convoy Escort Fleet was formed but its assets were little more than nominal. Based in Saipan and responsible for the Japan–Saipan, Saipan–Truk and Truk–Palau routes, the Second Fleet had only four destroyers to do the work.

Shipping losses mounted through 1943. After July 1943 they would never be less than 100,000grt per month and around August of that year it finally began to penetrate the consciousness of the naval staff that something was seriously wrong. Captain Atsushi Oi joined the naval staff in July 1943:

> If I remember right it was about 20 August 1943 that we first realised that some innovation had come to American torpedoes. The sinking rate of our torpedoed ships suddenly began to increase. Furthermore since the previous spring our shipping losses had reached a far higher level than ever before.[2]

Shipping losses for September were 172,082grt, the highest figure for one month during the war. The more realistic elements in the Japanese High Command began to understand that Japan's lines of communication were ridiculously overstretched and, in particular, it was felt that the outer line of Rabaul and the Bismarck Archipelago could not be defended for much longer. Amid much recrimination about loss of honour, the Japanese agreed to retreat to a line stretching from the Marianas, through the Carolines to western New Guinea. It appears to have been the Japanese Army that was insisting on this rationalization of Japanese commitments rather than the Navy. Captain Oi remembers sitting in as an observer at a meeting between Vice-Admiral Seiichi Ito, a Vice-Chief of the Naval Staff, and his Army equivalent, Lieutenant-General Hikosaburo Hata. Ito was reluctant to countenance any withdrawal but Hata argued that the shipping situation was so serious that it would soon be impossible to hold Rabaul anyway. This new realism was reflected in the August 1943 decision that all merchant ships were henceforth to be escorted. At the same time a number of other schemes

---

[1] J. Winton, *Convoy: The Defence of Sea Trade 1890–1990* (London: Michael Joseph, 1983), p.313.

[2] A. Oi, *Why Japanese ASW Failed: The Japanese Navy in WW2 in the Eyes of Former Imperial Japanese Naval Officers* (Annapolis: US Naval Institute), pp.397–8.

were introduced to encourage Masters, by means of bonuses, to make quick passages and to carry as much cargo as possible. In March 1944 the load-lines on Japanese merchant vessels would be raised, permitting more cargo to be carried.

However, the most important step was the setting up of the Grand Escort Command on 15 November 1943 under Admiral Koshiro Oikawa, a former Navy Minister and one of the Navy's ablest commanders. Oikawa was made independent of the Combined Fleet and had authority over local commanders in matters of routeing, ASW and the salvage of merchant vessels. Yet once again the Navy's reluctance to allocate sufficient assets meant that Oikawa's task was hopelessly compromised before it had begun. His escort forces numbered fewer than fifty ships of 800 tons or above and included some old destroyers which were so unseaworthy that they were incapable of making an ocean passage. His best ships were four destroyers built in 1920–25 but only four of them had worked together as an escort group. All the rest were individual ships cobbled together from local commands. There was no common tactical doctrine and there were no common communications procedures. Equipment was generally obsolete if not old, for, as ever, the Combined Fleet had first call on new items. The personnel were decidedly second rate and skilled technical ratings were in short supply. Any officer or rating who showed promise was either drafted into the Army or the Combined Fleet. It did not augur well for success.

The convoy system begun by Oikawa came into full operation in January 1944. Convoys were small by Western standards, five to eight ships per sailing being the usual number. A twenty-ship convoy was unusual, but one such, which included three fleet oilers and was protected by an escort carrier and twelve other escort vessels, was reported in the Manila area on 20 August 1944. It was subsequently attacked and twelve of the merchant ships were sunk.

At the start convoys were too numerous to be escorted adequately by the escorts available. Later the number of escorts increased, owing to the constriction of the convoy routes as the Americans advanced. Nevertheless, even with this improvement there were not enough escorts, and sinkings continued as long as there were ships afloat to sink. Sinkings in November 1943 exceeded 300,000 tons and in January 1944 went over the 350,000-ton mark. For the remainder of 1944 such falls as there were in the monthly figures were due to the Americans' diverting their submarines and aircraft to other tasks. In March and April 1944 there were falls in the tonnage sunk by submarines of about 50 per cent due to the submarines' being required to support the Fleet in the Central Pacific. Throughout the summer of 1944 the sinkings of Japanese ships by American aircraft also fell as the carrier task groups were switched to supporting amphibious operations. However, once the aircraft were released in September 1944 the figures began to rise again. The total of 3,892,019 tons of Japanese shipping sunk in 1944 was so large that Japanese industry, working flat-out, could not make good half the losses (new construction in 1944 being 1,699,203 tons) and consequently the Japanese merchant fleet declined by two million tons—equivalent to almost 50 per cent of Japan's pre-war fleet.

The convoy system reached its peak in the middle of 1944 but from then routes were progressively abandoned as the Americans rampaged across the Pacific (see Table 12). The routes between Rabaul and Truk and the Marshalls and Truk had to be given up almost as soon as they were set up. Palau, the assembly point for eight convoy routes, was abandoned in August 1944 in anticipation of an American assault which became a reality the following month. After that date, apart from coastal convoys along the west coast of the Philippine archipelago, the important convoys from the oil port of Balik Papan to Surabaya for onward routeing to Singapore and convoys from Surabaya to the Kendari air base in the southern Celebes, no Japanese ships in the south Pacific were routed east of the meridian of Manila, all on account of a lack of escorts. In the autumn of 1944 the routes from Saigon to Miri and Manila were abandoned for lack of escorts. Other routes such as Singapore–Miri, Takao–Hong Kong and Shanghai–Takao were given up for lack of merchant ships, especially tankers. Moji–Shanghai convoys were abandoned in January 1945 and until American submarines forced the Japanese out of the Yellow Sea in June 1945 all shipping sailed independently using pre-arranged routes. In October 1944, after the American conquest of the Philippines, the convoys in the South China Sea were reorganized in 1944. The tanker convoys northwards were maintained until March 1945, by which time the losses had become so great that the Japanese ceased to send empty tankers southwards to load. The Singapore–Palembang/Saigon route was never abandoned though losses became severe. The protection of convoys in the open sea in the end became so difficult that ships hugged the coast, keeping within soundings where submarines could not operate and under such air cover as could be provided.

However, the Japanese did not react entirely passively to the decimation of their merchant marine. The US attacks in the China Sea were a particular cause for concern and as a result the Japanese Army and Navy issued joint instructions for convoy protection. Convoys were to be larger, for more effective use of the escorts, and air cover was finally recognized as being of prime importance: pilots in air units assigned to trade protection duties were to have intensive training in night flying. It was tacitly admitted that morale in merchant ships had fallen as a result of the high level of sinkings and steps were taken to improve this. Escort ships were warned to keep a better lookout and to ensure the more efficient use of anti-submarine devices after nine escorts were sunk in May and early June.

On 3 August 1944, after American submarine activity in the China Sea was threatening to disrupt communications, the Japanese decided to reorganize the Grand Escort Command. Admiral Kischsaburo Nomura, who had

TABLE 12: JAPANESE CONVOY ROUTES[3]

Route	Date abandoned	Reason
Truk–Marshall Islands	Dec 1943	Allied carrier raids
Truk–Rabaul	Dec 1943	Allied landings at Cape Gloucester
Palau–Hollandia	Jan 1944	Attacks by land-based aircraft
Moji-Shanghai (direct)	Jan 1944	Escorts required for Japan–Formosa route (ships travelled unescorted thereafter)
Palau–Truk	Feb 1944	Abandonment of base at Truk obviated need for oil from Borneo
Japan–Palau	Feb 1944	Shortage of escorts (route replaced by direct Formosa–Palau route)
Morotai–Biak	May 1944	Fall of Biak to Allies
Surabaya–Ambon	May 1944	Air threat from Biak
Saipan–Truk/Palau/Japan	June 1944	Capture by Allies of Saipan
Balik Papan–Manila	June 1944	Submarine menace in Sulu Sea and Celebes
Takao–Palau (direct)	June 1944	Convoys re-routed via Manila
Manila/Davao/Balik Papan–Palau	Aug 1944	Expectation of amphibious assault on Palau
Takao–Hainan	Aug 1944	Shortage of shipping and reduction in iron ore imports in favour of more urgently needed bauxite
Hong Kong–Hainan	Aug 1944	Shipping more urgently needed on Singapore routes
Davao–Halmaheera	Sept 1944	Occupation of Morotai
Manila–Saigon	Sept 1944	Shortage of escorts
Singapore–Medan	Oct 1944	Submarines in Malacca Strait and shortage of escorts
Saigon–Miri	Nov 1944	Shortage of escorts
Miri–Manila	Nov 1944	Attacks from Leyte-based aircraft
Singapore/Surabaya–Balik Papan	Nov 1944	Air raids from Morotai
Manila–Ormoic/Davao	Nov 1944	Air raids from Leyte
Singapore–Miri	Jan 1945	Shortage of tankers and obstruction of anchorage at Singapore by sunken ships
Singapore–Rangoon	Jan 1945	Threats from submarines
Takao–Hong Kong, Shanghai–Takao, Moji–Takao	Feb 1945	Shortage of shipping
Takao–Singapore, Kyushi–Singapore	Feb 1945	Expected assault on Okinawa or Formosa
Tokyo–Bonin Islands/Osaka	Mar 1945	Expected losses from Iwo Jima-based aircraft
Moji–Tsintao/Dairen	June 1945	Attacks from Okinawa-based aircraft
Moji–Shanghai (diversive Yellow Sea route)	June 1945	Operation 'Barney'

relieved Oikawa in July 1944, was now placed under the command of the Grand Fleet. It is hard to see any sort of rationale behind this decision. If the planners in Tokyo felt that the CinC Combined Fleet might be tempted to release some his assets for convoy protection then they were mistaken. If anything the boot was on the other foot and escort ships found themselves being used for fleet operations.

---

[3]Admiralty: Naval Staff History, *War with Japan, Vol. 5: The Blockade of Japan* (London, 1957), pp.149–50.

Other 'reforms' included the disbandment of the Second Convoy Escort Fleet and the redesignation of the First, now under the command of Vice-Admiral F. Kiishi, as a task force for escorting long-distance, high-value convoys. Forces allocated to Kiishi now consisted of three groups of escort vessels, named the 101st, 102nd and 103rd Squadrons, to which the 105th was added on 10 July 1945. A further development was the formation of a special anti-submarine force for the Luzon area in the Philippines. At various times in 1944 eight escort groups were formed, although these existed on paper only—no forces were ever allocated to them. Escorts were still allocated to convoys on an *ad hoc* basis depending on availability: the dedicated escort groups of the British Western Approaches Command with their sophisticated support, analysis and training facilities simply did not exist in the Far East. These measures, limited though they were, did have some effect. As early as the spring of 1944 Admiral Lockwood was concerned by the heightened Japanese anti-submarine activity, which was responsible for a worrying increase in the number of boats failing to come back from patrol. Obviously the Japanese were learning something from experience and submarine operations were becoming more difficult and hazardous.

One area of Japan's seaborne trade which was of special concern was the import of oil and petroleum-based products. The beginning of the war caused a considerable increase in the demand for tankers since the conduct of the war meant a huge increase in oil and petrol consumption. The oilfields lay at the furthest reaches of the Empire and, since foreign-flag tankers were no longer available for charter, the Japanese had to rely on their own fleet, new construction, conversions from dry cargo vessels and captured enemy tankers. In 1942 conversions from dry cargo vessels had provided most of the new tonnage, but from 1943 onwards the effects of new construction were felt, 375,000 tons coming forward in that year, with a 50 per cent increase in the next fiscal year (see Table 13).

Japan's tanker tonnage rose throughout the war until January 1945, after which a rapid decline set in. By the end of the war Japan had barely over a quarter of a million tons' worth of tankers left, of which, it is claimed, only one-third was operational.

The offensive against Japanese tankers developed slowly. In 1942 only two tankers were sunk. This was because of a lack of American submarines. The oil routes from Palembang to Singapore and Japan and from Surabaya to the Combined Fleet base at Truk via Balik Papan were a considerable distance from the submarines based at Fremantle in whose operational area they lay, and until 1944 only eight submarines were available. There were few tankers to be found in the China Sea until the oil wells destroyed by the retreating Allies were repaired. In the Manadated Territories the situation was little better, the Americans relying on submarines in transit from Pearl Harbor to Brisbane to patrol the area. It should also be realized that tankers were faster than the average dry cargo vessel and the slow 'S' class submarines which

72. USS *Puffer*, a *Gato* class boat, has a spectacular sideways launch at Manitowoc Shipyards on the Great Lakes. American submarines were frequently built far inland and shipped to the ocean by canal.

73. Above the control room was the conning tower containing the attack instruments.

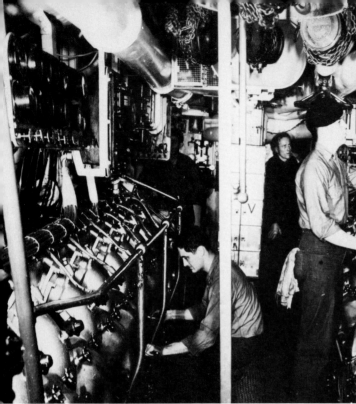
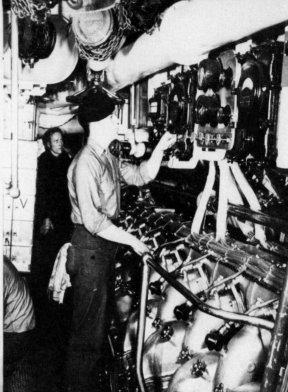

▲74

74. The engine room. With the exception of the HOR engine, American machinery was well designed and practical.

75. The crew space in a fleet boat, larger and more comfortable than comparable spaces in submarines of other navies.

76. The spacious and well equipped galley: American submariners ate well on patrol.

▼75　　　　　　　　　　　　　　　　　　　　　　　　　　　　76▶

▲ 77   ▼ 78

77. The torpedo space, with a seaman's bunk fitted in above two Mk XIV torpedoes.

78. A Mk XIV torpedo fitted with the troublesome Mk VI exploder erupts against the cliffs at Kahoolowe, Hawaii, during trials ordered by Admiral Lockwood.

79. An American submarine tender with three of her charges. Excellent repair facilities and logistics kept the submarine force at sea.

▲ 80   ▼ 81

80. A Japanese 'C' type *Kaibokan, No 17*. Note the depth-charge racks at the stern.
81. A 'D' type *Kaibokan, No 8*, outside Nagasaki in February 1944.
82. A Japanese battleship fires her main armament during a peacetime shoot. Planning for the descisive naval action obsessed the Japanese.

82 ▲

83. Officer cadets at the Etajima Naval Academy study navigation. Trade protection and the usefulness of convoy were not on the syllabus.

84. A *Fubuki* class destroyer damaged by *Wahoo* in a 'down the throat' shot at Wewak in 1943.

85. Lt-Cdr Dudley 'Mush' Morton with his executive officer, Lt Richard O'Kane, on the bridge of USS *Wahoo*.

85▼

BOW BUOYANCY TANK

FR. #4

7

▲86

86, 87. Damage to *Growler*, sustained in her collision with the *Hayasaki* on 7 February 1943.
88. The old destroyer *No 39* sinks after being torpedoed by *Seawolf* on 23 April 1943.

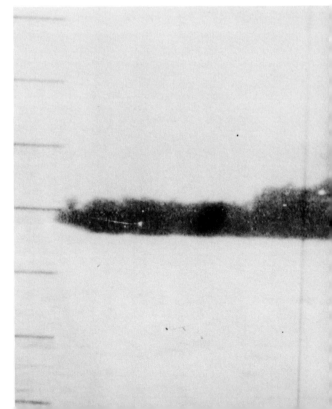

87▲   88▼

▲89

▲90　▼91　　　　　　　　　　　　　　　　　　92▶

89. *Takachiho Maru* heads for the bottom after being torpedoed by *Kingfish* on 19 March 1943.

90. USS *Tautog*—the top-scoring American submarine in terms of the number of ships sunk, with twenty victims.

91. Cdr Howard Gilmore, awarded the Congressional Medal of Honor for sacrificing his own life to save his submarine, USS *Growler*.

92. Lifeguard duty: Lt-Cdr Richard O'Kane of USS *Tang* and the twenty-two airmen he rescued at Truk in April 1944—a record number.

93. Cdr Eli T. Reich of USS *Sealion* (II), who sank the battleship *Kongo* on 21 November 1944.

94. Members of *Sealion*'s ship's company pull former Allied prisoners of war aboard following the sinking of the liner *Rakujo Maru* on 12 September 1944. American submarines picked up 159 of the prisoners.

95. Lockwood awards the Navy Cross to Cdr Eugene Fluckey of USS *Barb* in August 1945.

▲93　▼94

95▶

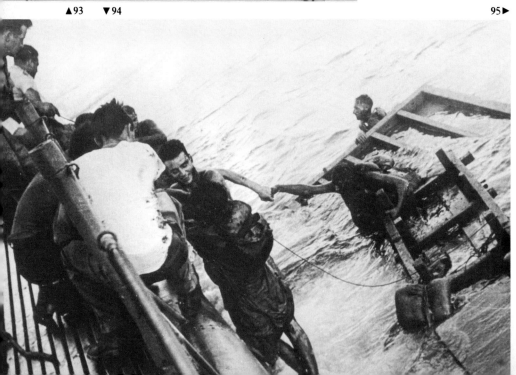

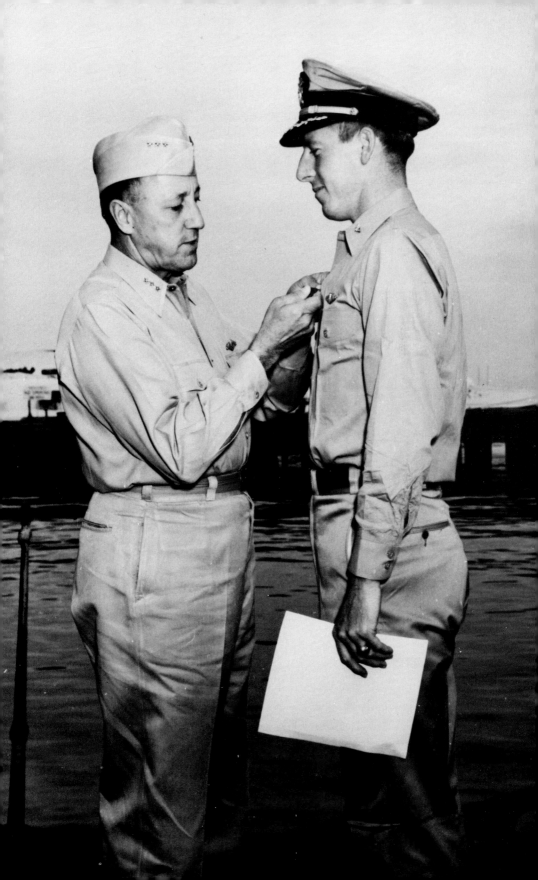

96. End of the road: USS *Sailfish* pays off at the end of the war.

TABLE 13: JAPAN'S TANKER TONNAGE, 1941–45[4]			
Year	Tonnage afloat	Losses (tons)	Net gain/loss
1942	587,000	9,000	+99,000
1943	686,000	175,000	+186,000
1944	873,000	824,000	−12,000
1945	861,000	362,000	−594,000
15.8.45	267,000		

made up the bulk of the South West Pacific Fleet were at a considerable disadvantage when trying to catch one. American efforts against the tanker fleet were also compromised by differences in policy in the various theatres. In the South Pacific area tankers made priority targets for US submarines after warships as early as 1942, but in the Central Pacific area tankers were classed after battleships, carriers and cruisers in order of priority. It was not until early 1944 that the South West Pacific boats joined in a concerted offensive against tankers.

However, in 1944 the attacks on tankers began to have an effect. Submarines alone were not responsible: 85,000 tons' worth of tankers were sunk during the massive air attacks on Truk (February 1944) and Palau (March 1944). Construction was stepped up until one-third of Japan's shipbuilding capacity was taken up with tanker construction. The rate of new construction doubled during 1944 so that by the beginning of 1945, when dry cargo tonnage had been virtually halved, tanker tonnage was still at its maximum.

Yet despite the prodigious efforts made by the Japanese shipbuilding industry to replace lost tonnage, by early 1944 the Combined Fleet, the Air Arm and industry were all suffering from a shortage of oil and related products. In the spring of 1944 the Combined Fleet moved to Singapore so as to be nearer the sources of supply. In no single year during the war did Japan's imports and oil exceed 50 per cent of the average for the ten pre-war years and stocks declined from 20 million barrels in December 1941 to 200,000 barrels in March 1945 when the last tanker got through. Imports ceased thereafter. When the battleship *Yamato* sailed on her one-way operation against American forces at Okinawa in 1945, dockyard officials were reduced to emptying the bunkers at the dockyard using a chain gang of sailors to dredge the bottoms so as to give the ship enough fuel.

The number of tankers was clearly inadequate, yet the total tonnage did not show a significant decline until 1945, so what was wrong? As ever, the Combined Fleet was the major culprit in that, having insufficient fleet oilers, it requisitioned 20 per cent of the civil fleet until it abandoned Truk in 1944. Moreover, the lack of suitable storage facilities at many Japanese bases meant that a significant number of tankers were tied up (literally!) acting as fuel

[4]*Ibid.*, p.97.

stores. Lastly, the route through the China Sea on which the Japanese depended for most of their oil imports suffered more than any other through loss of efficiency in that evasive routeing away from areas in which US submarines were known to be operating was employed, together with other tactics such as hugging the coast and anchoring at night. The net effect of these measures was that a ten-day voyage could take up to three weeks, thus making very inefficient use of the available assets.

In the December quarter of 1944, when shipping was finding the passage of the China Sea a hazardous enterprise, a peak 2,000,000 tons of tankers were engaged in importing oil into Japan, yet the amounted actually imported was no more than 217,000 tons. In that quarter of the year one tanker was being sunk every other day. The Japanese authorities realized the seriousness of the situation and made strenuous efforts to bring in oil. A report written at the end of 1944 for the Cabinet by the Total Mobilization Bureau stated:

> The preservation of communication between the southern occupied territories and Japan is absolutely necessary for the maintenance of national material strength. It is recognised that if the resources of the south, especially petroleum, are abandoned, as time passes we shall gradually lose our ability to resist attack.[5]

After the South China Sea route was abandoned in March 1945, Japan had to rely on resources from the Inner Zone, but these constituted no more than one-sixth of Japan's *peacetime* requirements. Various stratagems such as importing oil in submarines and manufacturing it out of sweet potatoes and apples were resorted to but they could not compensate for the loss of the oilfields in the south.

Meanwhile factors were at work which were to reduce the tanker tonnage afloat at the beginning of 1945 by an average of 150,000 tons a month. The need to import food meant that tankers were now being converted to dry cargo vessels—318,000 tons of tankers were lost thus between January and August 1945 while new construction ceased after March 1945. Whole convoys were being wiped out for lack of escorts, particularly air cover, while the establishment of air bases in the Philippines by the Americans rendered passage of the China Sea virtually impossible. In response, the Japanese tried to lessen the loss rate by splitting the convoys into groups of no more than three ships and by giving them as much defensive armament as possible. The passage of these last convoys resulted in a virtual massacre. Thirty-four tankers were sunk in January 1945 (fourteen of them on one day, the 12th), nine in February and fifteen in March when the last tanker convoy got through to Japan.

The decision to abandon the China Sea in March 1945 was not taken lightly: the Japanese realized that it meant abandoning the vast resources of

---

[5]*Ibid.*, p.102.

the south which they had gone to war for in the first place. The steady rate of attrition of Japanese shipping through US submarine attack was the main reason, although the effect of US carrier operations, and in particular the devastating ten-day raid carried out in the China Sea between 10 and 19 January 1945, was important. The Japanese also felt that the invasion of Okinawa of Formosa (or both) could not be long postponed, so they resolved to bring all their remaining shipping into the Sea of Japan behind the Home Islands. Here Japanese shipping sailed on a peacetime basis with no escort and with navigation lights burning. But in June 1945, in Operation 'Barney', this last refuge was breached.

The experience of the last convoys to brave the China Sea was not a happy one. On New Year's Eve 1944 a convoy left Japan for Singapore to bring back oil. It consisted of six tankers, four dry cargo vessels, eight escorts and the fleet oiler *Kamoi*. Off Formosa two tankers and two cargo ships fell victim to submarines and *Kamoi* and two escorts were damaged by air attack. One escort then broke down and quitted the convoy. Off Hainan island the convoy returned to Hong Kong since American carriers were in the area. Aircraft from these carriers attacked the convoy the next day in Hong Kong harbour, sinking three tankers and the remaining two cargo vessels and damaging *Kamoi* and three or four of the escorts so badly that they had to drop out. The convoy, now consisting of three or four escorts with one tanker, was attacked by a submarine off Malaya and one escort was badly damaged. On 24 January 1945, 25 days out from Japan, the 'convoy' arrived at Singapore. The remaining tanker, *Sarawak*, then struck a mine in the channel and sank.

The decision to abandon the South China Sea was an admission of failure by the Japanese: their convoy system had not worked. The Japanese had failed to integrate their air and surface forces with the movement of convoys. Convoys had successfully protected British shipping in the Atlantic against a scale of attack far greater than that experienced by the Japanese. Yet Japan's adoption of convoy failed to have any effect on merchant shipping losses. There are several minor contributory factors in this, such as the inefficient operation of merchant shipping, but the overriding reason is the lack of escorts and, above all, of air cover. Most convoy routes, especially those in the South China Sea, were ringed by Japanese air bases, and the failure to provide air cover was inexcusable. Perhaps the most damning verdict on the failure of the Japanese convoy system comes from the official British history of the blockade of Japan:

Summing up, the primary reason for the failure of Japan's convoy system to protect her shipping lay in her failure to provide adequate air and surface escort and in her total failure to exploit her shore-based aircraft. There was also a failure to organise and operate her aircraft and surface vessels efficiently, to operate her convoys on a cycle consonant with their escort availability and to provide forces in sufficient number and efficiency to be effective fighting components of the convoys they escorted. The number of escorts ought to have been one of the main planning factors determining the composition, frequency and speed of convoys. The Japanese Naval Staff did not cut its coat according to the cloth available—in fact, the indications are that they did not understand the first principles of organising a convoy system scientifically.[6]

---

[6]*Ibid.*, p.105.

CHAPTER NINE

'Now Get Out There and Give 'Em Hell!'

It is inevitable that we will crush you before we are through with you. — Admiral
Harold Stark USN

*Pursue relentlessly . . . do not let cripples escape or leave them to sink—make sure
they do sink.* — General Instructions for Seventh Fleet Submarines

A T THE BEGINNING of 1943 the Americans had a force of eighty
fleet boats in the Pacific. After the successful conclusion of the
Guadalcanal Campaign in February 1943, the Americans began to
withdraw their submarines from the South West Pacific theatre. At the same
time patrols off Truk, Palau and the Marshalls were considerably reduced.
The boats thus released joined forces with those already operating from Pearl
Harbor in waters around Japan and in the South China Sea. By the second
quarter of 1943 nearly three times as many submarines were employed in
these waters as in the first quarter. During the summer and autumn of 1943
nearly half the submarines in the Pacific Fleet were employed on the trade
routes to and from Yokohama, Kobe, Nagasaki and other large Japanese
ports, mainly those south of Tokyo.

Another change in 1943 was brought about when Admiral English was, as
we have seen, killed in an air crash. His place was taken by Admiral
Lockwood from Fremantle, who in turn was replaced by the newly promoted
Rear-Admiral Ralph Christie, hastily recalled from the Torpedo Station at
Newport, Rhode Island, where he had been sent to sort out the delays in
torpedo production. As the forces of General MacArthur pushed northwards,
so the operational areas available to the Brisbane boats decreased rapidly.
Consequently Fife's force was reduced from twelve to eight boats, the four
surplus boats going to Fremantle where they would be joined by another
dozen, bringing Christie's force up to 24.

Lockwood's appointment to Pearl Harbor saw an improvement in the way
that submarines were deployed. Whereas in 1942 only 15 per cent of patrols
had been directed against 'Empire' waters, in 1943 the percentage had risen
to 50 and for the first time he began to exploit the bottleneck in the Luzon
Strait. Likewise Christie and Fife gave up stationing their boats off known
Japanese anchorages and instead deployed them seaward along trade routes.
An increase in the number of submarines available was one reason for the
different dispositions, as was the winding down of military adventures in
Guadalcanal and the Aleutians, but a realization among the various force

commanders of the importance of blockading the Empire was a significant factor.

Improved dispositions by the force commanders were matched by the increased aggression shown by submarine commanding officers. Only 14 per cent of commanding officers were relieved for 'low productivity' in 1943 as opposed to 30 per cent in 1942. One of the first commanding officers to show what the Americans were going to achieve in 1943 was Lt-Cdr Dudley Morton USN of USS *Wahoo*. Morton had taken over *Wahoo* after her previous commanding officer had been relieved for 'low productivity'. He inherited a discontented and disprited crew but by sheer force of personality, which earned him the nickname 'Mush', he welded them into an efficient fighting unit. On his first patrol from Bisbane Morton disabled a *Fubuki* class destroyer in a daring 'down the throat' shot during an excursion into Wewak harbour in New Guinea. The destroyer had been lying at anchor when her lookouts spotted the tracks of *Wahoo*'s torpedoes but then followed the tracks, intending to drop a depth charge pattern. 'In order not to lose the initiative we continued to be aggressive', wrote Morton.[1] Two days later *Wahoo* engaged a Japanese convoy off New Guinea and sank two cargo ships and a transport. She sent the following signal to Pearl Harbor:

> In ten hour running gun and torpedo battle destroyed entire convoy of two freighters, one transport, one tanker . . . all torpedoes expended . . . returning home.[2]

The morning after this action Morton found another convoy. With no torpedoes on board and only forty rounds of 4in ammunition, *Wahoo* went after the merchant ships, hoping to collect a straggler and sink her with gunfire. However, the Japanese ships had seen the submarine and had summoned help in the shape of a destroyer which proceeded to put her down and carry out a fairly ineffective depth charge attack for the best part of an hour. When the coast was clear Morton surfaced and made his now immortal signal to Lockwood: 'Another running gunfight . . . destroyer gunning . . . *Wahoo* running'.[3]

This was the sort of thing Lockwood wanted to see. When *Wahoo* returned to Pearl Harbor she had a broom tied to her shears and Morton received the Navy Cross from Lockwood and an Army Distinguished Service Cross from General MacArthur. However, there was another side to this otherwise successful patrol which illustrates one aspect of the war at sea which was peculiar to the Pacific. During the convoy action off New Guinea *Wahoo* came across several small boats each containing a considerable number of armed Japanese soldiers who were survivors from one of the ships he had

---

[1] T. Roscoe, *United States Submarine Operations in World War II* (Annapolis: US Naval Institute, 1949), p.205.

[2] *Ibid.*, p.206. The tanker sinking was not confirmed by JANAC.

[3] *Ibid.*, p.207.

sunk. Morton ordered the guns to be manned, the boats shot up and the soldiers killed. To some this was a repugnant act but Morton's superiors, judging from the glowing endorsements on his patrol report, were not over-concerned. The war in the Pacific was a racial conflict. The Japanese were perceived as barbarians whose brutal excesses against prisoners and civilian populations only spurred the Americans on in their determination to defeat them. Morton continued to wreak havoc among Japanese shipping until he, together with his submarine and ship's company, were lost in October 1943 in La Pérouse Strait.

Another incident during the early part of 1943 served as an inspiration for up-and-coming US submariners—the selfless action of the commanding officer of USS *Growler*, Lt-Cdr Howard Gilmore USN. Gilmore was an aggressive officer who had gained recognition in the Aleutians Campaign when he attacked three Japanese destroyers off Kiska, sinking two and damaging the third. On the night of 7 February 1943 he engaged the 900-ton cargo ship *Hayasaki Maru*. The merchant ship turned to ram *Growler* but the submarine failed to notice her alteration of course and, despite last-minute manoeuvring, the two ships collided at 17kts. The Japanese ship raked *Growler*'s bridge with small-arms fire, killing the Assistant Officer of the Deck and a lookout and badly wounding Gilmore. Gilmore ordered the bridge to be cleared prior to diving but when he found that he was unable to descend the ladder down to the control room because of his wounds he gave the order 'Take her down!' *Growler*'s executive officer, Lt-Cdr A. F. Schade USN, hesitated, but discipline and training prevailed and *Growler* dived. The submarine was not out of danger for she was riddled with bullet holes and thirty-five feet of her bows were bent back like cardboard, but Schade made temporary repairs and successfully brought the boat back to Brisbane, where his conduct received a ringing endorsement from Fife. Commander Howard Gilmore was not forgotten for he became the first American submariner to be awarded the Congressional Medal of Honor. The citation read:

> For distinguished gallantry and valor, above and beyond the call of duty . . . In the terrific fire of the sinking gunboat's machine guns, Commander Gilmore, refusing safety for himself, remained on deck while his men preceded him below.[4]

During 1943 the three Commands had together conducted about 350 patrols in total, about the same number as in 1942, sinking, according to post-war records, 335 ships totalling 1.5 million tons. These sinkings seriously impeded Japan's ability to import raw material. Imports showed a sharp drop, of nearly three million tons, between 1942 and 1943. Moreover, Japanese shipbuilding was not keeping up with the loss rate, as shown in Table 14. However, in terms of tankers alone the picture was more satisfactory. Japan began the year with 686,000 tons of tankers but in spite of

---

[4]*Ibid.*, p.208.

TABLE 14: LOSSES OF JAPANESE SHIPPING AGAINST NEW
CONSTRUCTION, 1943[5]

Month	Losses (tons)	New construction (tons)
January	158,885	12,549
February	92,662	42,954
March	147,540	107,444
April	132,724	16,838
May	134,661	31,315
June	105,108	48,000
July	84,361	63,966
August	100,064	62,483
September	178,966	88,805
October	158,093	80,412
November	320,807	87,278
December	207,048	126,041
Total	1,820,919	768,085

losing 150,000 tons she was able to increase her fleet, by means of new construction, salvage and conversion, by another 177,000 tons. This was despite an offensive, albeit belated, against tankers in the South China Sea by Christie's Fremantle boats. Though some of his submarines had carried out spectacular patrols only twelve tankers had been sunk.

As in 1942, considerable effort was still being spent on pursuing major units of the Combined Fleet. There were roughly sixty contacts between submarines and Japanese capital ships—ten contacts with battleships and the remainder with aircraft carriers. The majority of these attacks resulted in nothing more than frayed nerves or a depth-charge hammering from the Japanese. The small aircraft carrier *Chuyo* was the only major Japanese unit to be sunk by US submarines in 1943: she was torpedoed on 4 December by *Sailfish* (Lt-Cdr R. E. M. Ward USN). Only two Japanese submarines fell victim to their US counterparts: *I-24* to *Trout* (Lt-Cdr A. H. Clark) on 9 September 1943 and *I-182* to *Scamp* (Lt-Cdr W. G. Egbert USN) on 27 July 1943.

Another development in 1943 was the introduction of the 'wolfpack'. Once sufficient submarines became available, Lockwood decided to see if their capabilities could not be maximized by their acting together. In October 1943 the first 'pack', consisting of *Vero*, *Shad* and *Grayback* under the tactical control of Cdr 'Swede' Momsen, worked in the East China Sea, sinking three ships totalling nearly 24,000 tons. In November the second group, consisting of *Snook*, *Harder* and *Pargo* under the control of Cdr Freddie Warner, sank seven ships of 32,000 tons in the Marianas. A third pack, *Halibut*, *Haddock* and *Tullibee*, revisted the Marianas but sank only a 500-ton netlayer.

Opinion was by no means unanimous on the 'wolfpacks': submarine commanders disliked them because their freedom of action was limited and

---

[5]*Ibid.*, pp.523–4, and Admiralty: Naval Staff History, *War with Japan, Vol. 5: The Blockade of Japan* (London, 1957), p.97. The figures include those for tankers.

because they had to take along a divisional commander from the staff who would attempt to co-ordinate tactics. Moreover, with friendly submarines manoeuvring in close company in a confused tactical situation, they lived in constant fear of fratricide. Their arguments were supported by the successes of individual boats who collected scores equalling that of the 'pack': in September 1943, for example, *Trigger* sank 26,000 tons of Japanese shipping on her own in the East China Sea.

Communication between the boats was the chief problem. Momsen advocated stationing the tactical commander ashore, which would avoid having the boats use TBS (Talk Between Ships) to keep in touch with each other. As a result American 'wolfpacks' were never the tightly controlled formations adopted by the Germans in the Atlantic but resembled loose groupings of boats whose activities would be determined by the personalities of their commanding officers as much as by anything else. Co-ordinated search to increase the number of sightings (which would then be dealt with by individual boats) rather than concerted attacks was the theme.

As the American submarine offensive increased in tempo, then so did the extent and effectiveness of Japanese anti-submarine measures. During 1943 another fifteen US submarines did not return from patrol. Four boats, *Argonaut*, *Amberjack*, *Grampus* and *Triton*, were from Fife's Brisbane command, *Grenadier*, *Grayling*, *Cisco* and *Capelin* were from Fremantle and the remaining seven, *S44*, *Pickerel*, *Runner*, *Pompano*, *Wahoo*, *Corvina* and *Sculpin*, were from Lockwood's Pearl Harbor command. *Amberjack*, *Argonaut*, *Cisco*, *Corvina* (the only US submarine to be sunk by a Japanese submarine during the war), *Grampus*, *Grayling*, *Grenadier*, *Pickerel*, *Pompano*, *Runner*, *S44*, *Sculpin*, *Triton* and *Wahoo* were all sunk by Japanese forces—ships, aircraft or submarines—although there is doubt about the fate of *Pompano* and *Runner*, while *Capelin* was almost certainly mined. There were no survivors from these boats except for *S44*, *Grenadier* and *Sculpin*.

The end of *Sculpin* is worthy of special mention for her loss was the occasion for an act of unique heroism. *Sculpin* (Cdr Fred Connaway) was one of the submarines from Pearl Harbor tasked with supporting Operation 'Galvanic', the assault on the Gilbert Islands. Also on board the submarine was Captain John Cromwell, who would direct operations if a group of three submarines on station in the Truk area (*Sculpin*, *Searaven* and either *Apogon* or *Spearfish*) were to combine to form a wolfpack. On 18 November 1943 *Sculpin* encountered a Japanese convoy but was detected and forced deep while making her approach. Despite sustaining minor damage, she renewed her attack but was again sighted and forced deep. During the depth-charge attack which followed, *Sculpin* porpoised in full view of the enemy, who renewed his attacks with vigour. Eventually Connaway decided that he would surface and fight it out with his gun armament, but as *Sculpin* surfaced she was overwhelmed by a withering fire from the Japanese destroyer *Yamaguno*. Accordingly, the order to abandon ship was given, but Cromwell remained in

TABLE 15: JAPANESE SHIPPING LOSSES, 1944[6]

Month	Merchant ships sunk	Tonnage	New construction (tons)
January	50	355,368	108,216
February	54	518,697	124,902
March	26	263,805	256,450
April	23	128,328	83,183
May	63½	259,591	162,239
June	48	278,484	142,382
July	48	251,921	106,612
August	49	295,022	101,888
September	47	419,112	185,221
October	68½	512,378	144,675
November	53½	421,026	149,831
December	18	188,287	133,604
Total	548½	3,892,019	1,699,203

the control room. He was under no illusions that his knowledge of the operational use of 'Ultra' by the Americans and the details of 'Galvanic' might be extracted from him under torture and so resolved to ride *Sculpin* down to the bottom—along with twelve others of the crew who chose not to become Japanese prisoners. Cromwell was posthumously awarded the Congressional Medal of Honor. By a cruel twist, *Sculpin's* survivors were embarked in the aircraft carrier *Chuyo*, which was sunk by *Sailfish* on 4 December 1943. It was a particular irony because it was *Sculpin* which had stood by *Sailfish*, then called *Squalus*, when the latter had sunk accidently on 23 May 1939 off Portsmouth, New Hampshire.

In general, 1943 was the year in which US submariners learned how to fight a submarine war and received the equipment to do it. The commanders, Lockwood, Christie and Fife, were now much more experienced and aware of the limitations of the forces under their command. Supported by a superb staff organization ashore, including the brilliant Cdr Dick Voge USN and his superlative analytical techniques, they devised new tactics, including the wolfpack. The submarine commanders were younger men who had seen combat as executive officers and were not as bound by peacetime theory as their predecessors. By the end of the year the torpedo problems had been overcome and boats were going on patrol with a full load of torpedoes which worked as they were intended to. Radar was exerting an important influence on tactics, as was the example set by successful commanders like 'Mush' Morton, Sam Deleay and Dusty Dornin. Submariners were beginning to believe that their contribution to the war effort was substantial rather than peripheral.

The year 1944 saw the offensive have a considerable impact on Japan. During the year, allowing for losses, the number of operational submarines in the Pacific went up by thirty-three. The advance of the American amphibious forces through the Central and South West Pacific meant that new bases, for

[6]Roscoe, pp.523–4, and Admiralty: Naval Staff History, p.97.

example Milne Bay, Manus, Mios Woendi, Majuro, Saipan and Guam, became available. The acquisition of these bases drastically reduced the time spent on passage. More boats, more bases and smaller operational areas— these would be important ingredients for success in 1944.

The twin campaigns in the Central and South West Pacific would see the submarines diverted to other duties such as screening for the American carrier task groups, patrolling known operating areas of the Japanese Fleet and lifeguard duty (rescuing downed aviators). It was, however, against Japanese commerce that their main efforts would be directed. Lockwood and Christie mounted 520 war patrols, sinking more ships than in 1941, 1942 and 1943 combined (see Table 15). These losses had a serious effect on Japan's merchant marine. Excluding tankers, her tonnage was reduced from 4.1 million tons to 2 million tons. Tanker tonnage actually increased during the year, from 863,000 tons to 869,000 tons, but to maintain this level the Japanese shipbuilding industry had to build 204 ships of 624,000 tons—proof of the havoc the American submarines were wreaking.

The submariners themselves were becoming more confident and daring. At the end of January 1944 Cdr Slade Cutter USN in *Seahorse*, operating north of Truk, had a battle with a convoy with was an epic of dogged persistence. On 28 January 1944 Cutter spotted three freighters closely escorted. He tracked the convoy for thirty-two hours before he was able to attack, and his first salvo of three torpedoes sent the 2,747-ton *Toko Maru* to the bottom. Throughout 30 and 31 January Cutter tailed the convoy and at 0019 on 1 February he was able to engage again. However, his first two salvoes missed, because of the convoy's erratic movements. With only two torpedoes remaining and his crew exhausted after a chase which had lasted over 80 hours, Cutter ordered a submerged attack using his SJ radar, with all three escorts only 1,500yds away. This time he was more fortunate and the 4,004-ton *Toei Maru*, loaded with gasoline, blew up and sank. USS *Tang*, under the command of Lt-Cdr Richard O'Kane, who had been Morton's executive officer in *Wahoo*, was another boat which made her mark on the Japanese. During her first patrol she sank five ships of 21,400 tons.

In March 1944 Lockwood sent a three-boat wolfpack to the Luzon Strait. The three boats were *Parche* (Lt-Cdr 'Red' Ramage), *Bang* (Lt-Cdr Anton Gallaher) and the veteran *Tinosa* (Lt-Cdr Donald Weiss). The three boats sank seven ships of 35,300 tons: Gallaher got three ships of 10,700 tons, Ramage sank two of 11,700 tons and Weiss collected the remaining two totalling 12,900 tons.

One of the roles allotted to US submarines was the blockade of islands about to be, or being, invaded by the Americans. In this, three submarines did useful work in preventing the arrival of Japanese reinforcements. On 26 April 1944 USS *Jack* (Lt-Cdr Tommy Dykers) sank the *Yoshida Maru*, which was carrying 3,000 Japanese troops bound for New Guinea. There were no survivors. Lt-Cdr Jimmy Dempsey in USS *Cod* found the same convoy off

Luzon and sank one escort, a 7,200-ton transport, and damaged two others. Thus the two submarines had prevented the best part of a Japanese infantry division from being sent to New Guinea.

In May 1944 Lockwood sent a wave of his submarines into the Marianas to prevent the Japanese from reinforcing their garrisons prior to the American assault on the islands. *Silversides* (Lt-Cdr John Coye) was spectacularly successful, sinking five ships. Into the same area Lockwood sent a pack consisting of *Pintado* (Clarey), *Pilotfish* (Close) and *Shark* (II) (Blakely), under the operational control of Cdr Leon Blair in *Pintado*. The 'pack' assumed the nickname 'Blair's Blasters', thus starting a fashion for naming the pack after the senior officer coupled with an appropriate sobriquet. 'Blair's Blasters' lived up to their name for they attacked four convoys and sank seven ships totalling 35,000 tons. Though many of the troops survived, their equipment went straight to the bottom. The troops which did reach the Marianas thus arrived late, without their equipment, and could not be integrated into the defensive plan.

The summer of 1944 was dominated by the Battle of the Philippine Sea, that curious and complicated engagement in which neither fleet sighted the other. The American submarines played a useful role in the battle, being deployed off Japanese fleet anchorages. *Redfin* (Lt-Cdr Marshall Austin) sighted and reported the Japanese fleet leaving Tawi Tawi, as did *Flying Fish* (Lt-Cdr Robert Risser), but neither boat was unable to attack. On 19 June, the day of the 'Marianas Turkey Shoot', US submarines made their own mark on the Japanese by sinking two carriers. *Albacore* disposed of *Taiho*. Damage to the Japanese ship was not serious at first, but inadequate damage control completed Blakeney's handiwork: the damage control officer ordered all watertight doors open to allow petrol fumes to disperse, but instead they filled the ship, turning her into a floating bomb with the predictable result that *Taiho* was torn apart when the fumes ignited. The second carrier victim was *Shokaku*, veteran of Pearl Harbor, Coral Sea and Midway, which was torpedoed by Hermann Kossler's *Cavalla* on the submarine's first patrol.

After the Philippine Sea battle, Lockwood and Christie flooded Japanese waters with submarines. Although boats continued to operate individually and were successful in doing so, greater emphasis was placed on wolfpack operations, sufficient submarines now being available to make such groupings practical. Wolfpack techniques had developed considerably since the early haphazard efforts in 1943. It was now found best to allow boats to attack independently. Only the broadest tactical directions, such as the disposition of his boats as 'flankers' and 'trailers', were given by the senior officer. Searches, however, were closely co-ordinated and usually conducted at night when the submarines' high speed and radar could be used to the best effect. A submarine making contact with the enemy would call up her colleagues and shadow or attack immediately. After attacking, the submarine would use her superior speed to make an 'end around' to get ahead of the convoy and be in position for another attack. Such tactics were very effective, and since the Japanese had no radar, there was very little they could do to combat them.

In May/June *Barb* (Lt-Cdr Gene Fluckey) and *Herring* (Lt-Cdr David Zabriskie) were sent into the Sea of Okhotsk. Fluckey had promised Lockwood that he would sink five ships, and he proceeded to do exactly that—*Koto Maru* and *Madras Maru* on 31 May, *Toten Maru* and *Chihaya Maru* on 11 June and *Takashima Maru* on 13 June. Fluckey later recalled that

> Admiral Lockwood reminded me that, by God, I was the only skipper during the war who told him exactly how many ships he was going to sink and then went out and did.[7]

Barb's running-mate, *Herring*, was less fortunate. It was Zabriskie's second patrol and he was keen to do well, having received a roasting from Lockwood for an unproductive first trip. In an attack on the harbour at Matsuwa, he sank the *Iwaki Maru* and *Hiburi Maru* on 1 June; but that was to be all, for the submarine was engaged by shore batteries, hit and sunk.

Seahorse, under the command of the veteran Slade Cutter, constituted a one-boat pack on her own, sinking four ships in the Luzon Strait between 27 June and 4 July 1944. Of her pack-mates *Growler* and *Bang*, the former sank one ship before having to return to Midway for lack of fuel and the latter sank nothing. It was the last patrol for Cutter: he returned to the United States on leave and was then assigned to a new construction. JANAC assessed Cutter as having sunk nineteen ships, which put him in joint second place with Morton in the list of top-scoring US submarine COs. He had an awesome ability to find Japanese shipping and was relentless in pursuing their destruction. Lockwood jested that Cutter could find a 'Maru' in Pearl Harbor if he wanted to.

In July and August 'Donk's Devils', comprising *Spadefish*, *Redfish* and *Picuda* under the command of Cdr G. R. Donahoe USN, worked the Luzon Strait and sank thirteen ships totalling over 55,000 tons, making them the most productive pack of the war. In August *Ray*, *Haddow*, *Guitarro* and *Raton* engaged a twelve-ship convoy with five escorts in a running fight which went the length of the South China Sea, sinking five ships totalling 28,000 tons despite almost continuous air cover and coast-hugging tactics by the convoy.

During the summer of 1944 Japanese shipping losses averaged 200,000 tons per month. In October there were 43 boats on patrol and they sank 68 ships with one shared kill. Most of the Japanese losses occurred in their reinforcement of the Philippines (where aircraft were particularly effective in the anti-shipping role) and in the South China Sea and the waters around Formosa, where the wolfpacks enjoyed complete superiority and were able to

---

[7] C. Blair, *Combat Patrol* (Bantam Books, 1978), p.293.

sink 50 or even 75 per cent of the ships in a convoy. Between May and December 1944 some sixty wolfpacks operated, but it is important to remember that the independent submarine could, and did, sink as many ships as a pack.

In November 1944 Guam was opened as a submarine base, thus giving Lockwood's boats another four days in their operating area. As the Japanese perimeter contracted in the face of the relentless American advance, so their sea lanes became confined to the East China and Yellow Seas. After the fall of the Philippines, Lockwood's boats concentrated exclusively in the waters around Japan while Christie's boats cleaned up in the South China Sea and the waters around Singapore. Merchant ship losses tailed off in December as there were so few targets available, but a pack consisting of *Flasher*, *Hawkbill* and *Becuna* disposed of four tankers and a destroyer in the South China Sea in December. Their total of 42,868 tons made them the highest-scoring pack.

During 1944 American submarines sank 548 Japanese ships amounting to 3,892,019 tons. They had, however, been unable to exceed an average attrition rate of 1.5 ships per month for every boat in the operational area, with one in three attacks proving successful. This was because, by the end of the year, there were 156 submarines in the Pacific and with the smaller operating area there were too many boats chasing too few targets. Although a comparison with the Atlantic theatre shows that the American submarines were sinking less than the German U-boats, the Japanese merchant marine was much smaller than the British merchant fleet and so the losses were proportionately greater. Another million and a half tons of shipping were sunk by other agents, mainly aircraft, during 1944 and since 3 million tons of shipping was required for Japan's civilian needs alone, it was clear that the end was in sight.

The year 1944 also proved to be good for submarine successes against Japanese warships. The score amounted to one battleship (*Kongo*), seven carriers (*Shokaku*, *Taiho*, *Taiyo*, *Unyo*, *Jinyo*, *Shinano* and *Unryu*), nine cruisers (*Agano*, *Tatsuta*, *Yubari*, *Oi*, *Nagara*, *Natori*, *Maya*, *Atago* and *Tama*) and about thirty destroyers. *Kongo*, the only Japanese battleship to be sunk by a submarine, was engaged by *Sealion* (Cdr Eli T. Reich USN) on 21 November at the northern end of the Formosa Strait. *Sealion* picked up the Japanese force, which consisted of the battleships *Kongo* and *Haruna* escorted by two cruisers and three destroyers, on radar shortly after midnight and Reich decided to make a surface attack—despite the bad weather, which was causing solid waves to break over *Sealion*'s bridge. He fired three Mk XVIII electric torpedoes at *Kongo* from his bow tubes and then three Mk XVIIIs from the stern tubes at *Haruna*. He saw three hits on *Kongo* but was not to know that his salvo against *Haruna* had missed but had taken the destroyer *Urakaze* instead. The battleships continued their course and Reich was disappointed that he had, apparently, only damaged the battleship. He chased after the force, ignoring the heavy weather and hoping to make another attack. Before he could do so, he noticed that *Kongo* was losing way and dropping astern. Suddenly there was a

> . . . tremendous explosion dead ahead . . . sky brilliantly illuminated, it looked like a sunset at midnight. Radar reports that battleship pip getting smaller, that it had disappeared.[8]

Perhaps the most surprising submarine success against a Japanese capital ship was the loss of the giant aircraft carrier *Shinano* to *Archerfish* (Lt-Cdr Joseph Enright). Enright was a cautious commanding officer who had previously asked to be relieved of command of *Dace* because he lacked confidence in himself. On 29 November he was on lifeguard duty off Tokyo Bay when he stopped the giant carrier, sister-ship to the super-battleships *Yamato* and *Musashi*, heading south. *Archerfish* raced after her at flank speed and was only able to keep up because the carrier's zigzag allowed the submarine to draw slowly ahead. Suddenly *Shinano* turned towards *Archerfish*, presenting Enright with almost the perfect target. Six torpedoes were fired and four hit the carrier. Although the damage was not serious, it was compounded by poor damage control and *Shinano* later sank. There was some scepticism when Enright claimed a 28,000-ton *Hayatake* class carrier but, backed up by his divisional officer (none other than Cdr Klakring, formerly of *Guardfish*), the sinking was awarded to him. It was not until after the war that the identity of Enright's victim was known and he was eventually given the credit and belatedly awarded a Navy Cross.

The reverse side of this catalogue of success is that nineteen US submarines failed to return from patrol. Lockwood lost thirteen boats, *Scorpion*, *Grayback*, *Trout*, *Tullibee*, *Gudgeon*, *Herring*, *Golet*, *Shark* (II), *Tang*, *Escolar*, *Albacore*, *Scamp* and *Swordfish*, and Christie lost six, *Robalo*, *Flier*, *Harder*, *Seawolf*, *Darter* and *Growler*. *Seawolf* was a victim of mistaken identity by US forces; *Tang*, an outstandingly successful submarine under the command of Lt-Cdr Richard O'Kane, and *Tullibee* were victims of their own torpedoes which circled back; *Darter* went aground and was abandoned, having been shelled by *Nautilus* to prevent the Japanese obtaining anything useful from her; and *Robalo* was the victim of a battery explosion. The remainder were all victims of Japanese ASW forces or minefields. The Exchange Rate, that crucial figure in commerce warfare, was one US submarine to every 42 ships. In addition, three submarines, *Barbero*, *Halibut* and *Redfish*, were withdrawn from front-line service because they were so badly damaged.

In 1945, sinkings fell as the Japanese were pushed even further back towards the Home Islands (see Table 16). The liberation of the Philippines meant that the South China Sea was closed as far as the Japanese were concerned and this route was abandoned along with all communications with such southern territories as remained to them.

---

[8]*Ibid.*, pp.348–9.

When convoys were found they were attacked ruthlessly. The case of convoy MO-TA-30 is a perfect example of the havoc one wolfpack could wreak. The convoy consisted of eight merchant ships escorted by a destroyer and eight or more smaller escorts. On 8 January 1945 it was *en route* from Moji in Japan to Formosa and then onward to Singapore when it was attacked by 'Loughlin's Loopers' consisting of *Queenfish* (Cdr Eliot Loughlin), *Barb* (Lt-Cdr Gene Fluckey) and *Picuda* (Lt Cdr Ty Shephard). *Barb* opened the action at 1723, firing three torpedoes and scoring one hit on the 10,000-ton *Anyo Maru*, which broke in half before sinking. Another torpedo from this salvo hit the 9,200-ton *Shinyo Maru*. At 1725 *Barb* fired a further three torpedoes, two of which hit the 7,500-ton *Sanyo Maru*, which blew up, the explosion being observed by *Queenfish*. At 1915 *Queenfish* fired ten torpedoes at three ships but observed no hits. *Picuda* joined the action at 1954, scoring one hit on the 7,600-ton *Hikoshima Maru*. Another torpedo from this salvo hit the sinking *Shinyo Maru*, which was finally finished off by three torpedoes, heard running by *Picuda*, from *Barb*. The ship disappeared in a huge explosion. At 2150 *Queenfish* fired four torpedoes and got hits on the 10,000-ton *Manju Maru*. In the same attack the 2,857-ton *Meiho Maru* was hit, reversed course and was later abandoned. No maritime power could survive this sort of savage assault for long.[9]

In the last few months of the war targets became fewer and fewer and submarines were spending more and more time on lifeguard duty. Lockwood resolved to send his boats into the Sea of Japan, an area which had been neglected by US submarines since *Wahoo* was lost there in 1943. The operation, known as 'Barney', was to be the last major sortie by the US submarine force. For the dangerous passage through the minefields in the Tsushima Strait the submarines were fitted with clearing wires around their propellers and bow and stern planes, but more importantly they were fitted with short-pulse active FM sonar which would give a visual presentation of any minefield. Nine boats (*Seadog, Crevalle, Bonefish, Tunny, Tinosa, Skate, Bowfin, Flying Fish* and *Spadefish*), under the command of Cdr E. T. Hydeman in *Seadog* and glorying in the name 'Hydeman's Hellcats', were fitted for this operation and began running through the Tsushima Strait into the Sea of Japan from 3 June 1945. All the boats made the passage safely though *Tinosa* and *Skate* heard mine cables scraping down their sides. In order to allow all the boats to reach their widely scattered patrol areas, operations were not to commence until 9 June, by which time all the boats would be on station. The early arrivals had to exercise self-control.

It was a spectacularly successful operation. The submarines found Japanese traffic sailing independently and showing lights. In the next seventeen days they sank 27 surface ships and a submarine. The only

---

[9]'The Confusing Case of Convoy MO-TA-30', *The Submarine Review* (Alexandria, Va: Naval Submarine League, July 1989).

TABLE 16: JAPANESE MERCHANT SHIP LOSSES, 1945[10]

Month	No of Ships	Tonnage
January	22	93,796
February	15	55,746
March	23½	70,727
April	18	60,696
May	32	32,394
June	43	92,267
July	12	27,408
August	4	14,559

unfortunate incident was when *Spadefish* sank a Soviet ship north-west of La Pérouse Strait. On 24 June the surviving eight boats (*Bonefish* having been sunk on 19 June off Honshu by a patrol boat) safely exited on the surface together through La Pérouse Strait while the submarine *Trutta* carried out a diversionary bombardment of the island of Hindo Shima.

A second wave, consisting of *Sennet*, *Piper*, *Pargo*, *Pogy*, *Jallao*, *Stickleback*, and *Torsk*, repeated the operation in July and August and mopped up what was left of the traffic, and on 14 August *Torsk* sank the escort vessels *13* and *47* and in doing so fired the last torpedoes of the Second World War.

During the Second World War US submarines sank almost 55 per cent of Japanese shipping, both naval and merchant—1,152 ships, totalling 4,859,634 tons. This figure was achieved by a force numbering no more than 2 per cent of the US Navy's manpower. America lost 52 submarines, with 374 officers and 3,131 enlisted men killed. Casualties in the submarine force were proportionally higher than in any other branch of the service. 'The atomic bomb was the funeral pyre of an enemy who had been drowned', wrote Theodore Roscoe in his summation of the American campaign. The crux of the matter is that American submariners had strangled Japan's economy and in a sense rendered the dropping of the atomic bomb in 1945 unnecessary:

> The holocaustal incandescence which consumed Hiroshima and Nagasaki could not blind observers to the fact that the maritime empire was already destroyed. And long before the first mass air raids smote Tokyo, many Japanese-held harbours in the SW Pacific were as deserted as the bays of the moon, and in many of Japan's home seaports there were vacant docks with rusting bollards where only spiders tied their lines . . .[11]

---

[10]Roscoe, pp.523–4, and Admiralty: Naval Staff History, p.97.

[11]Roscoe, p.495.

CHAPTER TEN

Conclusions

Those who cannot remember the past are condemned to fulfil it. — George
Santayana

WHAT CONCLUSIONS can be drawn from this study of two
campaigns in which submarines were used to blockade and starve
the other belligerent into surrender? The conclusion is a simple
one: convoy provides the only means of protecting maritime trade in time of
war. Any other method of protection hands the initiative to the aggressor.

In the First World War Britain suffered massive losses as the U-boats
roamed at will in the waters around the British Isles and in the
Mediterranean. Losses continued to rise until it seemed that the predictions
of the German *Admiralstab* might be fulfilled. However, once British
merchant shipping was placed under the protection of convoy, the U-boats
lost the initiative. Although they continued to sink considerable amounts of
shipping, it was the wrong sort of shipping. As convoy spread, the U-boats
were forced to ply their trade in areas not covered by the convoy system until
practically the whole of the area around the British Isles was excluded to
them. While they were chasing the odd independently sailing vessel, looking
for small coasters or spending considerable time in transit to distant patrol
areas off the American coast or the Azores, the procession of convoys kept
coming, each ship loaded with the supplies necessary to keep Britain and her
allies in the war.

The German Navy never succeeded in addressing the problem of how to
cope with the convoy system. The nearest it ever came to regaining the
initiative was the plan for a 'wolfpack'—a number of boats operating
together. The idea was sound, and indeed twenty years later it would come to
bitter fruition, but the communications available in 1918 made the idea
impracticable. Thus the Germans lost the initiative—and the battle. Convoy
provided the British with all these cardinal principles of war: offensive
action, security, concentration of force, economy of effort, flexibility, inter-
arm co-operation and an improvement in the morale of the men in the ships
being convoyed. The introduction of convoy thus gave Britain a low-key but
war-winning victory.

In the Pacific, twenty years later, it was a different story. The Japanese did
adopt convoy and they did so sooner than Britain did in the First World War.
Having done so, their merchant marine was still wiped out by the Americans.

If convoy represented a universal panacea, why did this happen? For the Japanese, convoy was not enough. For a number of reasons they did not appreciate the danger with which they were faced. When their convoy system was introduced it was half-hearted, denied of resources and scarcely efficient. The Japanese were also facing an enemy who was as ruthless as themselves (though in a different way) and one that was backed by almost limitless material resources which were beyond the reach of any of Japan's forces other than by a full-scale invasion of the US mainland. In this sense the Pacific campaign is unusual in that the *guerre de course*, traditionally the stratagem of the weaker power, was in this case used by the stronger one, although this probably was more a result of the circumstances surrounding the US entry into the war than any deliberate policy on behalf of the US Government.

The Americans achieved technical superiority with their radar and other equipment, despite the problems with torpedoes early in the war. These improvements gave the US forces the edge so that they were able to circumvent the Japanese convoys and engage them on their own terms, forcing the Japanese to route them away from known US submarine operational areas—the reverse of what happened in the Atlantic in the First World War. Convoy should have given the Japanese the same protection as it afforded Britain in the Great War (although whether it would have saved them from defeat is another matter). But it didn't. The Japanese never understood the convoy system and they neglected its principles, particularly inter-arm co-operation, and paid the price accordingly.

In the post-war period the art of convoy seems to have been forgotten. NATO strategists were fond of discussing protection of the 'sea lanes' and 'maritime lines of communication'. The reader of the naval press would learn of 'safe routes' and 'moving havens' for merchant shipping, all of which sounds terribly familiar to the student of convoy. Yet in the 1982 Falklands War and in successive crises in the Persian Gulf, modified forms of convoy have been used. The oft-imagined and written-about scenarios of convoy battles in the Atlantic between the Red Fleet and NATO will probably remain academic in view of the break up of the USSR. Nevertheless, naval planners would do well to remember the victory which the U-boats almost won in 1917 and the 'silent victory' won by the Americans in 1945.

BIBLIOGRAPHY

Admiralty: Naval Staff History. *War with Japan, Vol. 5: The Blockade of Japan*. London, 1957

Bacon, Admiral Sir Reginald. *From 1900 Onward*. London: Hutchinson, 1940

Bell, A. C. *History of the Blockade of Germany and the Countries Associated with Her in the Great War*. London: HMSO, 1961

Blair, Clay. *Combat Patrol*. Bantam Books, 1978

Compton-Hall, Richard. *The Underwater War*. Blandford Books, 1982

Dönitz, Karl. *Memoirs: Ten Years and Twenty Days*. London, 1959

Edwards, Lt-Cdr Kenneth. *We Dive at Dawn*. London: Rich & Cowan, 1939

Hashagen, Commander Ernst. *The Log of a U-boat Commander*. London, 1931

Jameson, Rear Admiral Sir William. *The Most Formidable Thing*. London: Hart Davies, 1965

Mahan A. T. *The Influence of Sea Power on the French Revolution and Empire*. Boston, 1894

Newbolt, Sir Henry. *Naval Operations*. 5 vols. London: Longmans, 1928

Oi, Atsushi. *Why Japanese ASW Failed: The Japanese Navy in WW2 in the Eyes of Former Imperial Japanese Naval Officers*. Annapolis: US Naval Institute

Spindler, Admiral Arno. *Die Handelskrieg mit U-booten*. 5 vols. Berlin, 1935

Tarrant, V. E. *The U-boat Offensive 1914–45*. London: Arms and Armour Press, 1989

Taylor, A. J. P. *The First World War*. London: Penguin Books

Terraine, J. *Business in Great Waters: The U-boat Wars 1916–45*. London: Leo Cooper, 1989

Roscoe, Theodore. *United States Submarine Operations in World War II*. Annapolis: US Naval Institute, 1949

Winton, J. *Convoy: The Defence of Sea Trade 1890–1990*. London: Michael Joseph, 1983

INDEX

Aircraft
employed against submarines, 37
British use of in support of convoy operations, 53
Japanese use of in support of convoy operations, 84–7
Albacore, USS
sinks Japanese cruiser *Tenryu*, 73
sinks Japanese aircraft carrier *Taiho*, 108
Anti-Submarine Division, formation of, 30
Arabic, SS
sunk by *U24*, 21
Archerfish, USS
sinks Japanese aircraft carrier *Shinano*, 111
Asahi
sunk by USS *Salmon*, 68
Asdic
British development and use of, 38
Japanese use of, 86
limitations of, 86
Atlantic Trade Convoy Committee, 49
Auxiliary Patrol, 33–4

Balfour, Sir Arthur, First Lord of the Admiralty
orders increase in number of escort vessels, 34
Balloons
employed against submarines, 37
used in sinking of *U69* by HMS *Patriot*, 37
Baralong
sinks *U27*, 36

Barb, USS
puts to sea with reconditioned torpedoes, 83
operations in the Sea of Okhotsk, 109
'Barney', Operation
participation in by US submarines in Sea of Japan, 112–13
Barrages
Dover 30–2
Otranto, 32
ineffectiveness of, 32
Bauer, *Fregattenkapitän* Hermann
views of on blockade, 16
plans for co-ordinated U-boat attacks on convoys, 62
Bayley, Vice Admiral Sir Lewis
appointed to Queenstown command, 35
Becuna, USS
as part of highest-scoring wolfpack, 110
'Blair's Blasters' (US submarine pack)
operations of, 108
Blockade
use of U-boats for blockade of Britain, 16
effects of British blockade on Germany, 28
Blum, *Kapitänleutnant* Ulrich
estimates number of U-boats required for a blockade of Britain, 16
Bremse, SMS
attacks Scandanavian convoy, 57–8
Brummer, SMS
attacks Scandanavian convoy, 57–8
Brussels, SS
captured by Germans, 43